$11.95

THE EXPERIMENTAL COLLEGE

Alexander Meiklejohn

LIKE REVOLUTIONARY EDUCATORS of every era, Alexander Meiklejohn believed that an undergraduate college must teach students how to think—about the social, political, and economic problems of their time. He wanted to make students—the lazy, the dim, and the exceptional—into thinking, caring, active citizens with the intellectual skills to participate in a democratically aspiring society.

In 1927, with the founding of the Experimental College at the University of Wisconsin, he had a chance to test and refine his original concept for a truly practical liberal arts program. *The Experimental College* is his chronicle of this experience.

During the educational and social upheaval of the late sixties and early seventies, many U.S. colleges acquiesced to student demands for the elimination of required coures. Individual fields of study—biology, journalism, engineering, and so on—became increasingly fragmented; the science and math studied by the biologists had nothing to do with the writing and editing of the journalists. In short, colleges were losing their ability to help students develop a general quality of mind and a set of intellectual skills that would make them in some shared way *educated.*

Now, academicians and, to some degree, business employers are finding that the product of a specialized education wears badly. Because a narrow range of experience inevitably becomes obsolete, the specialist lacks the basic intellectual capacities that make individual growth possible.

With this new edition, *The Experimental College* will once again become essential reading for educators, administrators, and future teachers who seek a philosophy and blueprint for a liberal arts curric-

*Alexander Meiklejohn at his desk.
Amherst College, 1912.*

THE

Alexander Meiklejohn

EXPERIMENTAL COLLEGE

Edited and Abridged
by John Walker Powell

SEVEN LOCKS PRESS, INC.
Cabin John, Md./Washington, D.C.

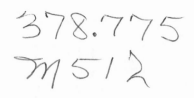

Copyright © 1932 by Harper & Brothers

Preface to the Seven Locks edition
Copyright © 1981 by the Alexander Meiklejohn
Experimental College Foundation

Library of Congress Cataloging in Publication Data

Meiklejohn, Alexander, 1872-1964.
  The Experimental College.

  Bibliography: p. 175.
  1. University of Wisconsin. Experimental College. I. Powell, John
Walker, 1904—. II. Title.
LD6130.M4   1981   378.775'84   81-9354
ISBN 0-932020-10-0   AACR2
ISBN 0-932020-11-9 (pbk.)

Frontispiece and backcover photographs
by permission of the Trustees of Amherst College
Book design by Chuck Myers
Typography by Susan Kelly

Manufactured in the United States of America

SEVEN LOCKS PRESS, INC.
An affiliate of Calvin Kytle Associates
P.O. Box 72
Cabin John, Md. 20818

Note: The unabridged edition of *The Experimental College* was published by
Harper & Brothers in 1932 and reprinted by Arno Press, Inc. in 1971.

"The rulers of the state have said that only free men shall be educated. But reason has said that only educated men shall be free."

Epictetus, Fifth Century, B.C.

"Our scheme of government and of life can succeed only if, in their more mature years, men and women will engage in careful, enthusiastic, and guided study of common values, common dangers, and common opportunities."

Alexander Meiklejohn
(1872-1964)

ulum that avoids too-early concentration on job skills (and its opposite, the rarified air of academic scholarship.)

Meiklejohn's report is as important for its careful description and dissection of the failures of the College as for its attention to the triumphs. Laymen, professional educators, and students alike will be fascinated by his passionate account; most astounding, though, is that today, fifty years after it was written, *The Experimental College* still speaks to us in a personal voice, educating us, inciting us to think, and urging us to join in the search for a deeply meaningful liberal education.

John W. Powell, age 23, at the
Experimental College

JOHN WALKER POWELL, abridger and editor of the Seven Locks edition of *The Experimental College*, was a founding member of the College faculty. After receiving his doctorate in philosophy and psychology at the University of Wisconsin, he followed Meiklejohn to teach at the San Francisco School of Social Studies where he later became director of the school and, finally, of the school's Sonoma County branch. The two men maintained their strong personal and professional ties until Meiklejohn's death in 1964.

Jacket design by Chuck Myers

SEVEN LOCKS PRESS
Cabin John, Md./Washington, D.C.

JOHN WALKER POWELL—teacher, writer, scholar, administrator, and consultant—began his close professional association and friendship with Alexander Meiklejohn while studying for his Ph.D. in philosophy and psychology at the University of Wisconsin. After working as Meiklejohn's assistant, he joined the founding staff of the Experimental College in 1927 and remained there for its duration.

In 1933, Mr. Powell joined Meiklejohn in San Francisco to help pioneer a new kind of adult education center. It became the School of Social Studies, the first—and only—adult group-study center under a full-time academic staff. He became director in San Francisco after 1935 and went on to become director of the Sonoma County branch of the school until 1942 when the war diverted funds and attention from liberal education.

Born in Duluth in 1904, John Powell attended Phillips Exeter at age fifteen, finished high school in Milwaukee and received his B.A. from the University of Wisconsin in 1926. Passionately committed to the need for better, more widely available adult education, Mr. Powell spent three years as director of Group Reading—a revolutionary experiment in adult education—under the auspices of the Washington, D.C. Public Library; worked for many years as a writer and editor for the Fund for Adult Education; and wrote the working paper for the 1960 White House Conference on Aging. During World War II he was director of community services (health, education, welfare, recreation, etc.) for the Japanese-Americans evacuated from California to Arizona War Relocation Centers.

Mr. Powell has taught at Harvard, The George Washington University, and Columbia. At the University of Miami, he created a new and unique intercultural program for freshmen and sophomores that focused on the humanities, history, and social science of Western and Eastern cultures. His many research projects include a year-and-a-half assignment exploring group-discussion patterns in mental hospitals and a socio-psychological study of responses to disaster. Mr. Powell now lives with his wife, the former Harriet Magdalene Morgan, in Washington, D.C. They have two children, Janet Swenson and John W. iv, and three grandsons.

Foreword

"One goes to college to learn how to think."

AMERICANS TODAY who never heard his name are nevertheless indebted to Alexander Meiklejohn—among other things for his pioneering efforts that brought adult education into the standard curriculum, and for his unfaltering championship of constitutional rights.

If republication of this book has its intended effect, we shall be in Meiklejohn's debt even more. For it is in these pages that he first laid out his stringent criticism of our colleges and universities, and most clearly articulated his own ideas about the purposes of a liberal education. At a time when these purposes are once again the subject of editorials, protest, and countless contentious studies, his ideas have renewed their power to inform, inspire, and provoke.

"It is worthwhile," he said in his inaugural address as president of Amherst College, "to acquaint boys with the sport of facing and solving problems." A friend who knew him in those days and who followed his career for the next fifty years says that Meiklejohn saw the college's task to be nothing less than "to enable its students to win the kind of reasoned, unified philosophy of life that can be brought to bear effectively on the problems of experience."* There was no confusion in Meiklejohn's mind. It was his simple

---

*Julius Seelye Bixler, "Alexander Meiklejohn and the Making of the Amherst Mind," *Amherst* 25(1973): 1-6.

conviction that one goes to college to learn how to think: "The college is the one agency specifically set apart by society for the training of the intellect." This apparently innocent belief made him one of the most controversial figures in twentieth-century education only because he tried earnestly—at Amherst, at the University of Wisconsin, and finally in San Francisco—to put it to work.

Meiklejohn was born in Rochdale, England, where his father, John, was a weaver and, not insignificantly for its impression on young Alec, an active member of the world's first permanent cooperative, the Rochdale Society of Equitable Pioneers. In 1880, when he was eight, the family moved to the mill town of Pawtucket, Rhode Island. Shortly thereafter, his father, a master of advanced weaving techniques and color design, became head of the color plants.

Meiklejohn attended public schools in Pawtucket and was graduated from Brown University in 1893. He later earned an M.S. from Brown and his Ph.D. from Cornell. He taught philosophy at Brown from 1897 to 1912, and served also as dean of the university, with particular reference to student counseling and guidance—a relationship his students cherished the rest of their lives. From 1912 to 1923 he was president of Amherst College where he continued to give his famous course in logic. ("Meiklejohn men up and down the country are readily identifiable," the late Robert M. Hutchins said of him on his seventieth birthday. "This is not because they agree, but because they think. They think about important things, and in such a way as to make other people think about them, too.") It was at Amherst, with the help of the textile unions in nearby Holyoke and Springfield, that he created the first adult education classes, teaching mill workers reading and writing, economics, and history. But after eleven years in the presidency his liberal policies—and to some degree his insistence that it was the trustees' duty to raise money and manage the campus budget, not his—led to such tensions that he felt impelled to submit his resignation; it was promptly accepted by the trustees. In what must have been one of the most dramatic commencements ever held, thirteen graduates of the class of '23 publicly refused their diplomas in protest.*

Three years later Meiklejohn was in Madison at the University of Wisconsin, where he had been asked to create and direct the radical teaching program that is the subject of this book. Although of enduring influence, it was a rather short-lived experiment, aborting in 1932 after "graduating" 327 devoted sophomores. Student performance varied, but no one touched by the experiment escaped a critical awareness of what a society is and how it works (or fails); and how its arts and sciences, its economics and politics, bear on each other and on the whole. A lifelong camaraderie bound most of the alumni to a Meiklejohn tradition, leading to frequent reunions and regional associations, and finally to an Alexander Meiklejohn Foundation dedicated to furthering his educational goals.

In 1933, Meiklejohn used the Experimental College's principles to create an adult education center, the San Francisco School of Social Studies. Like the Experimental College, the school offered no individual courses in specialized subjects but built its curriculum around a unifying theme, in this instance contemporary American society. Small groups of students, led by a member of the teaching staff, met weekly to discuss and debate the values and problems of American cities, particularly their own San Francisco. A reading list, dominated by books calculated to challenge their previously unchallenged views, included fiction and nonfiction, poetry and prose by the greatest thinkers in all fields. The program spread to rural areas in California, and was later adopted by libraries in major cities throughout the United States. Under auspices of the University of Chicago and St. John's College of Annapolis, Maryland, the format was adapted for nationwide exploitation in the Great Books adult study programs. By 1949 there were forty thousand Americans enrolled in adult study groups under a variety of public and private sponsors.

*For the definitive account of the Amherst incident, see Lucien Prince, *Prophets Unaware* (New York: The Century Co., 1924).

The motivating impulse behind all these developments, as it had been from his first teaching days at Brown, was Meiklejohn's unwavering belief in the obligation of citizens in a self-governing democracy to engage in continuous study of human societies and values. In one sense an idealist of the purest kind, he was in another a convinced pragmatist, insisting always that classroom inquiry was idle unless it was clearly relevant to social action.

A member of the National Committee of the American Civil Liberties Union for forty years, he became increasingly concerned with the Bill of Rights. In a memorable book written during the depth of the Depression, *What Does America Mean?*, he argued that the country's passion for "liberty" had blinded it to the real meaning of "freedom." It is freedom, not liberty, that lies at the heart of democracy, and he warned that we may be in danger of losing both. Our fetish of independence, he wrote, has permitted us to condone slavery, the betrayal of Indians and blacks, and "the humiliation of the spirit of women . . . the crowning insult which a society has offered to personalities of its own members." In 1963, in ceremonies at the White House, he was awarded the first Presidential Medal of Freedom.

Meiklejohn was among the first to champion intramural athletics and to attempt the organization of a league where college teams would meet rivals of their own strength. At Amherst, his efforts to de-emphasize intercollegiate sports were widely interpreted as indifference to the value of physical education. On the contrary, Meiklejohn himself was a superb cricket, hockey, and tennis player in his youth; he won a national bowling championship and was captain of the first American soccer team to beat a squad from Canada. It was not until he was eighty that his doctor limited his tennis playing to "doubles only." When he was ninety, few of his younger friends could keep up with him on his daily walks over the hills of Berkeley.

During his brief and final illness, at age ninety-three, Meiklejohn left his bed to draft a new constitutional amendment calling for federal subsidies for the education of all.

Foreword

When death suddenly and quietly overtook him, he was composing a letter to President Robert Sproul of the University of California, urging greater freedom for student protests.

IT IS THIS MAN—apostle of freedom, of intelligence, of self-government—that this book presents to the scrutiny of a new generation of teachers and students. Because the original volume was encumbered with the necessary details of university procedures and academic regulations, it has been abbreviated in this edition to its essential core. It is not a museum piece. It is a very living testament to an experience of vital importance to our own time. The college it describes was not an "experiment" in the loose sense we usually give to that word—meaning someone's attempt to do something he may not succeed in doing, or the taking of a chance to see how it will turn out. The Experimental College was *the* expression of a coherent and explicit philosophy about the meaning and purpose of human intelligence and human society. It was a belief testing itself in action, an *idea* hurling itself into the arena of life.

JOHN WALKER POWELL
Washington, D.C.
June, 1981

Contents

The Experimental College: Its Concept and Curriculum

CREATING A FRAMEWORK for the Experimental College was a difficult and challenging process for Meiklejohn and his "advisers" (the term given to the teaching staff). Each decision was the product of constant discussion, dissent and debate, and subject to modification based on new experience. Frequent changes in the personnel of the advisers introduced new talent and fresh ideas to the project. But despite changes and revisions, the heart of the original plan was sustained during the college's four-year existence:

A. The curriculum ran for two consecutive years. But, those two years were comprised of one single, consecutive full-time "course" in which *all students* and *all advisers* participated at the same times throughout each year.

B. The subject of the course was the nature and operation of a society, a "social order." For the entire freshman year, the example was fifth century Athens; for the entire sophomore year, contemporary American culture.

C. Each year's study was further divided into six-week segments. Each focused on one characteristic element of the culture under study: class structure, government, economics, literature, the arts, and philosophy.

D. Each student was required to read original works from the period and secondary texts about the society and the particular element of that society being studied; to write papers reflecting his perceptions and reactions;

to attend a weekly tutorial conference with his adviser for that segment (assignments were shifted at the end of each segment), as well as lectures by advisers (and guests) for his own class, and others for the college as a whole. Some advisers also held weekly meetings of their own group of advisees.

E. Lectures and readings were planned and given by the advisers expert in the field under study, but all advisers shared in the teaching of every subject. This did not mean that each adviser had to become an expert in every subject; his task was to bring his own total background and intelligence to bear upon the student's foreground in understanding what both were studying—the nature of a human society.

F. In 1928, a new element was added to the curriculum. Each sophomore student was required to make a "Regional Study" of a single American community (usually his own home town). This analysis of a community's make-up and ways of living helped the student learn to apply the kinds of thinking he had done about the Athenian civilization to something as immediate as the morning paper, as personal as his own back yard.

G. Finally, no grades were given until the completion of the second year—to meet the university's requirements and to determine each student's readiness to enter the junior year in the department of his choice: in Meiklejohn's words, "to establish not what he had done but what he is now capable of doing." During both years, however, each of his advisers reported his progress to his next adviser in a confidential memorandum. These comprised a total personal summary of the student's growth, which at the end of the two years was summed up in an oral examination by three other advisers.

These, then, were the elements of the Experimental College. Many were not unique. Shared dormitory living was not new. Students studying the same things at the same time was unusual but not unprecedented. Combining tutorial conferences with reading, writing, and lectures is common in Britain; and off-campus research periods had American counterparts. But here the comparisons ended—and the Meiklejohn innovations, which were the heart of the matter, took over. This was not the University of Chicago plan, nor the St. Johns plan (both of which came later, and had their own unique but different tenets). Here is Meiklejohn, himself, writing in the preface to the 1932 edition of *The Experimental College:*

> The positive term which this book uses in the attempt to fix the aim of education is "intelligence." Over against the training by which pupils are fitted for vocations, over against the instruction by which students are equipped with knowledge, is the liberal teaching, which attempts to create and to cultivate insight or intelligence. The term is not an easy one to define. . . . It is clear that into the meaning of the term there enter moral and aesthetic elements as well as intellectual.

> It is evident, too, that the idea implies unity of understanding as against the unrelatedness of scattered bits of knowledge. In view of what has already been said it may be assumed that the function of intelligence is to serve men in the creation and maintenance of a social order, a scheme of individual and group living, which will meet the human demands for beauty, strength, justice, generosity, and the like. But with these general remarks made, it will be best to let the term take on meaning as the deliberations of the advisers are described. These teachers have been trying to find out how young Americans can be made more intelligent. Insofar as they have succeded their success will appear in their clearer understanding of three main factors in the problem—first, what young men are and may be; second, what America is and may become; third, what is the human purpose which is seeking to find expression both in individual Americans and in the social

order which, for good or for ill, they are now creating.

Today, fifty years later, we can print these words again because nothing *basic* has changed. Once again, as it has done sporadically during the intervening years, this nation is reassessing itself and its purposes; and, again—and by the same necessity—it is doing so in part by a searching reevaluation of its own education: the goals, the methods, the content, of what its young people need to learn.

J.W.P.

The Experimental College
Alexander Meiklejohn

Edited and abridged by
John Walker Powell

I.

The Aim of the Liberal College

CHAPTER I

Intelligence and Scholarship

IF ONE IS DIRECTED to make suggestions for the improvement of a piece of work, the first question which he should ask is, What is the purpose of the work; what is it intended to accomplish? If, then, advisers are commissioned by a university to make suggestions for the improvement of liberal teaching in the first two years of the college course, their primary query must be, What does the university wish to get done by means of these two years of its instruction?

It is clear that to answer this question is to fix the place and the function of the two years in the larger scheme of education. Before entering the freshman class, students have already had some twelve years of formal teaching. After the close of the sophomore year, there are still awaiting them two later years of the liberal college course. And if these are finished, there are yet to come, for a few students at least, the technical or professional or graduate studies of the university. In a word, the freshman and sophomore years—which we may call the "lower college"—are not a closed and separate experience. They grow out of experiences which have gone before; they grow into experiences which are coming after. They are an episode within a continuous process of education. They can be understood only when they are seen as making their special contribution to that process as a whole.

If now, in the interest of simplicity of statement, we assume the lower college period to be in general that between eighteen and twenty years of age, the question at issue can be stated, externally at least, in numerical terms. What, in the course of their general development, should students learn between eighteen and twenty? What should they have learned before they are eighteen; what, between twenty and twenty-two; what, after they are twenty-two? To answer these questions would be, in a schematic way, to see, first, the primary and secondary schools, then the lower college, next the upper college, and finally the graduate school, each playing its part in a developing scheme of instruction. It would give us an ordered view of the educational ladder, from its bottom to its top. And with this accomplished we might then hope to see the lower college on its proper rung, in its proper relations to the teaching which has gone before and to that which is coming after.

The liberal college is usually defined in relation to the term *intelligence*. It intends to build up in a student the power of self-direction in the affairs of life. It rests upon the assumption, or the assertion, that over against the specialized teaching of men for banking, for scholarship, for industry, for art, for medicine, for law, and the like, there is the general liberal teaching of men for intelligence in the conduct of their own lives as human individuals. If, now, it be asked, "What is this 'intelligence' of which we speak?" we cannot do better than to borrow a phrase and a story from Abraham Flexner's recent stirring discussion of universities. "Long ago," Mr. Flexner tells us, "Germany learned that industry needs universities not merely because universities train chemists and physicists for research laboratories, but because universities train intelligence, capable of being applied in any field whatever. That lesson the American university has yet to learn."*

What, then, is intelligence as the term is used in defining the aim of a teacher? Mr. Flexner hits it off in many keen and telling phrases. The words just quoted, "intelligence, capable of being applied in any field whatever," give the essential meaning. One of its most delightful expressions is found in

---

*Abraham Flexner, *Universities: American, English, German* (New York: Oxford University Press, 1930), p. 177.

the telling of a story taken from George Herbert Palmer's *Life of Alice Freeman Palmer*. It recounts the difficulties and failure of Bridget, the cook, in the attempt to bake good bread. It then relates how Mrs. Palmer, untrained in cooking, came into the kitchen and created the loaf which, in that kitchen, had seem unattainable. Whereupon Mr. Flexner quotes with great admiration Bridget's definition of education. "That's what education means," she said, "to be able to do what you've never done before."* Bridget, it seems, saw at a glance and expressed in a word the peculiar quality of the educated, intelligent mind. But the delightful aptness of the story for our purposes is that, by her own test, Bridget placed herself at once with her mistress as in the same sense "educated." She, too, having never before, it is presumed, engaged in the difficult business of creating definitions of education, produced at the first stroke a masterpiece. She is not, evidently, supreme as a cook; she would not, one supposes, be highly rated as a scholar; but as a venturer into untried fields she is a startling success. And for that reason, she may well serve as a reminder to those who engage in the teaching of intelligence, that teaching is not the only means by which that quality is secured. But, however that may be, the primary fact is that in the story we find the meaning of the term *intelligence* as applied to teaching. Intelligence, it seems, is readiness for any human situation; it is the power, wherever one goes, of being able to see, in any set of circumstances, the best response which a human being can make to those circumstances. And the two constituents of that power would seem to be, first, a sense of human values, and second, a capacity for judging situations as furnishing possibilities for the realizing of those values. It is very near to "wisdom."

If now we seek to relate the college, as so defined, to the teaching institutions below and above it, there are two preliminary observations which must be made. The first has to do with numbers of students and the second with the

---

*Ibid., p. 159.

difference between general and special teaching.

One of the most striking features of the climbing procession of youth which makes its way up the educational ladder from primary school to university is that it is a dwindling one. The teaching enterprise which began at the bottom of the ladder, in the primary school, with millions of pupils, deals with only thousands at its final stage in the graduate school. At every step in the ascent, after the age of compulsory attendance is passed, multitudes of pupils disappear from the classroom, until at the end only a chosen and favored few remain. And, this being true, it is very dangerous to interpret the ladder only as it is seen from either of its ends. If this be done one may be sure that the activities at the other end will lose all their own proper quality and meaning. For the great majority who, at various stages in the process, leave the school to go into "practical" activities, the scholarly pursuits of the graduate school, which they will never reach, nor even approach, must be vague and meaningless. And on the other hand, if one's chief interest is centered in the higher ranges of scholarship, there is great danger that the lower schools will have meaning only as "preparatory," as leading the way toward forms of teaching with which, as a matter of fact, the education of the great mass of students in those schools has not the slightest concern. We must remember that, in the main, young people climb the first stages of the educational ladder, not with the purpose of making their way to the top, but in the expectation of finding beside the ladder here and there landing places from which they may climb by other ladders in other directions and toward quite different goals. And if these other goals and directions are not clearly seen in their relations to those of the school, then the whole scheme of teaching becomes unintelligible, a chaos of diverging and irrelevant activities.

The second observation is a classification of teaching activities into two radically different groups. In interest, in choice of material for study, some of our schools and colleges are "general," while others are "special." On the

6

one side, we find the teaching of the individual in the liberal, general sense. At many different levels, this enterprise is carried on. Its goal is the building up of the power of individual self-direction. It is trying to create or to cultivate "intelligence, capable of being applied in any field whatever." Each liberal institution, from the primary school to the college, takes charge, in turn, of this common task. Each, measuring the previous progress and capacities of the student, leads him as far as possible along the road which all are traveling.

But on the other hand, we have also a vast multitude of technical, vocational, professional, and research schools which are dominated by quite different sets of interest. They are concerned, not with the teaching of the individual in the general sense, but with the developing of his skill in some limited field of activity. If, for example, necessity compels a boy or girl of fourteen or fifteen to abandon general education, a business school may teach them commercial arithmetic, typewriting, and stenography. If young people of any age show taste and talent for music, they may be given over to teachers whose purpose it will be to cultivate this talent. And in the same way, schools of home economics, of agriculture, of engineering, of research in various forms, devote themselves, not to general education in personal power and understanding, except as these may serve the purposes of a special interest, but to the training of ability to ply a trade, to practice a profession, to master any one of the special enterprises in which human beings engage. Such schools are as multifarious as are the different occupations and activities into which human beings may enter.

The college can also be seen as the first of a series of increasingly specialized steps leading to the graduate school: more accurately, to one of the many separate graduate schools which carry to the highest level the formal instruction in law, medicine, science, theology, business—those many different fields of scholarship which vary as widely from each other as do the intellectual enterprises in which a cultivated and intelligent mind may engage.

But we must remember that not one in ten who enters a liberal college as a freshman will continue his studies to the graduate level. To put the matter quite bluntly, the college is as much—and as little—interested in the making of scholars as it is in the making of bankers, legislators, grocers, or the followers of any other specialized occupation or profession.

The college, it is true, does lay a foundation which will be of value. But that value is to be defined, not in terms of preparation for any of the callings or professions, but rather in terms of qualities of understanding and insight which in common are desirable for people of all callings.

And for that reason, no institution in our whole scheme of education is more deliberately, more persistently practical than the liberal college. Just as the trade school, the business school, the law school, and the school of agriculture prepare students for active life, so the college attempts to make its students more efficient, more successful in the activities of human living. Many of us believe that upon the achievement of liberal teaching depends the welfare of our social scheme—the possibility of saving it from disaster, the hope of making it a fitting expression of the human spirit.

CHAPTER TWO

The Lower College

THE PREVIOUS CHAPTER has defined abstractly the purpose of the liberal college. That college, we have said, intends, by using scholarship—its fruits or processes or both of these—to so cultivate and strengthen the intelligence of a pupil that he may be ready to take responsibility for the guidance of his own behavior. We must now see how, in actual administration, the college falls into two parts: the "lower" and the "upper" colleges. It will appear that the concrete situation is somewhat more complicated than our abstract statement has made it. We shall find that the first two years deal directly with the task defined, while the last two years seem to lead the way toward the new forms of activity which await a person whose capacity for taking responsibility has been established.

The function of the lower college is suggested, if not determined, by the fact that, for most of the students, it marks the time of their first "leaving home." In these two years, then, the pupil must learn, as his primary lesson, to take care of himself. In these years he comes to the end of formal lessons, given by teachers, in the understanding of himself and of his world of human facts and values. The time has come for his taking upon himself the responsibilities of maturity. Never again, unless he is taken over by a prison or a mental hospital, will any institution devote itself explicitly to the forming of his character, the general training of his mind, the enriching and directing of his personality.

In the years before his coming to college, home and school

have labored at this task. They have chosen his food, selected his underwear, arranged for his friendships, cultivated his tastes, guided his reading, formed his habits. In a word, they have taken responsibility for his making as a person. And through it all, if they have built wisely, they have been getting him more and more ready to take upon himself the responsibilities which, in the earlier years, they have perforce assumed. They have regarded him as a person who is being prepared to do for himself what, in ever-decreasing measure, his parents and teachers have done since his earliest childhood.

And now, somewhere about the eighteen to twenty period, as the student goes from home to college, the time has come for an explicit and avowed change of regime. If this be true, then all questions about instruction during this period, all questions as to the course of study, the methods of teaching, the determining conditions of life should be answered with reference to the successful accomplishment of that change of regime. The purpose of these studies is to help a young man in taking upon himself the responsibilities of being a man. Here, if our position is valid, is the principle for which we seek—a principle which might be used in the organization of the freshman and sophomore years. As such it defines the lower college.

We shall not understand this statement, nor use it with discrimination, unless we keep in mind the fact that other young people, who do not go to college, are, at about the same time, learning the same lesson. They too, at about the age of twenty, are expected to become free and responsible human beings, to put away the attitudes and thoughts of children, to become women and men. If we can remember this fact we shall not make the mistake of thinking that the fundamental lesson to be learned in a college is identical with the "studies" which we teach. Those studies are instruments peculiar to the college. But the lesson is common to all young people who are approaching maturity. It is being learned all about us by multitudes of young people—the Bridgets of Professor Palmer's story—who know nothing whatever either of colleges or of their studies. It is a general process of human learning of which our education by books and teachers is only a special limited phase.

It would help us greatly in remembering this fact if we could free ourselves from the mechanical terms which much of our thinking about education is done—if we could substitute for these, figures of thought taken from the field of organic growth and development. We seem to think of "studies" as if they were things to be taken into a student's system and kept there, unchanged, as permanent parts of his mental make-up. In this way we are accustomed to examine pupils to see whether or not what we have given them as mental food is still there, and, especially, whether it is still in the same form. One has only to carry over this procedure to the process of taking food into the body to see how inept and mistaken it is. The effect of healthily received food upon the body is measured, not by unchanging possession, but by the health and vigor and fineness of essential bodily activities. And the same is true of mental nourishment and care. Studies are not stuff to be acquired and kept. They are mental food to be used by an organism which, when they are not available, uses, under the normal conditions of life, quite different foods for essentially the same purposes. The analogy between mental and physical foods is not wholly exact. And yet it may illustrate our principle that, in the years between eighteen and twenty, the fundamental lesson to be learned cannot be fully expressed as the mastering of certain studies. Those studies are justified only as they serve the deeper purpose of fitting a young man or woman to face and to meet intelligently responsibilities which at that time inevitably come upon them.

When one says that the lower college marks the culmination of formal and explicit teaching in intelligence, that after the sophomore year a young man is no longer to receive direct instruction in matters of "wisdom," one does not mean to say that the college sophomore has already acquired all the insight which a human being needs. It is sometimes suggested that this interpretation of his achievement is characteristic of the sophomoric mind. And for him the mistake is a rather natural one. But, on the other hand, no one who has reflected upon the teaching of sophomores and has followed its consequences can long harbor such a misapprehension. What the principle means is, not that growth in intelligence is to stop, but that now it is to go on under the student's own direction. And the hope and presumption is that the process, having now reached the level of spontaneous self-expression, will proceed with greater speed and with greater certainty. Education in intelligence does not cease when it becomes self-education.

And now upon the basis of this statement we may perhaps determine with somewhat greater accuracy the relations of the lower college to the upper college and to the graduate school which, in many cases, follows it.

If we assume that in the lower college young people have learned, as it were, to stand on their own feet as they face life, what shall the upper college, the junior and senior years, offer them for purposes of further education? First, it may give them opportunities to further cultivate their minds by letting them search more deeply, in more scholarly fashion, into the processes of knowledge out of which the "wisdom" of the more general course has been derived. In these last two years the student may well explore how philosophy or science or literature is made; may try to get nearer to the minds of the masters in some one of these fields, to see how their creative work is done. The student will not in this way, nor in so short a time, become a scholar, in the graduate sense, but will achieve some fairly adequate view of what scholarship is, and so may come to better apprehension of the human spirit in its creative moods.

And second, the young person who has now won his freedom may well use that freedom for the making of a first significant decision. He must select, even though tentatively, his field of special interest and activity. He may, of course, if taste dictates or necessity requires, leave college and go at once to a shop, a farm, a studio, a railroad, an office. In this case he will find that the college has given him no special training for the work he is to do. He will take with him only such measure as he has won of "intelligence, capable of being applied in any field whatever." What little he has acquired of fact and of technique he will probably need to unlearn, or at least to learn differently, as quickly as possible. But, on the other hand, the student of twenty may, if conditions are favorable, choose to go into the upper college. And if we speak in human, rather than in financial, terms, his motive in so doing is fundamentally the same as that of others who have gone into "practical" activities: choosing a line of special work or interest and training himself to do it well.

CHAPTER THREE

Responsibility and Books

FOR EIGHTEEN YEARS a youth has been in process of liberal education. For twelve of these years he has been under the explicit guidance and direction of teachers who have sought to strengthen his grip on life, to fit him for the responsibilities which are now at hand. In this situation one might well expect that there would be running through the mind of every young person who is studying in a lower college some such thoughts as these:

> I hope that I may be judged ready to take my place as a free and responsible member of my community. I do not see at all clearly what I ought to be and do. Nor do I find it easy to form opinions on matters of public policy. In the modern world of value and of belief, problems of the greatest difficulty and of the greatest urgency wait for decisions which I cannot foresee. If, however, I am promoted to the level of intelligent self-direction and social participation, I will do my best to understand, to use my mind in the cause of under-standing. And I pledge myself that in action, in attitude, and in enjoyment I will follow unflinchingly such insight as I may be able to achieve. I ask, therefore, to be taught and then examined, so that it may be decided whether or not I am ready for my responsibilities.

Nothing could be more revealing of the present state of American culture and, therefore, of American education, than the fact that such words, if we actually heard them coming from the lips of a freshman or sophomore, would seem to us fantastic and ridiculous. Any boy found guilty of using them would be regarded by his comrades as a thing apart—a prig, a "square," an intellectual. The normal young American expects, and is led to expect, on his twenty-first birthday, not a new sense of responsibility, but a new automobile, a new set of opportunities for self-gratification. And it is in relation to that young American, and to the society which creates him, that the activities of our teaching go on.

And yet there have been times, and there are now countries, in which such expressions of attitude and purpose would not be held fantastic. In the Athens of the old days, a young man as he came to maturity was expected, and himself hoped, to take the ephebic oath:

> I will never disgrace these sacred arms, nor desert my companion in the ranks. I will fight for gods and home, both alone and with many. I will transmit my fatherland, not only not less, but greater and better, than it was transmitted to me. I will obey the magistrates who may at any time be in power. I will observe both the existing laws and those which the people may by agreement hereafter make, and, if any person seek to annul the laws or to destroy them, I will do my best to prevent him and will defend them, both alone and with many. I will honor the religion of my fathers. And I call to witness of my oath Agraulos, Enyalios, Ares, Zeus, Thallo, Auxo, and Hegemone.

But, however foreign it may be to our contemporary mood and situation, such a suggestion as that of the ephebic oath has value as pointing a direction, as setting a goal, in relation to which we may judge our present teaching arrangements or may estimate the merits of new ones which are proposed. It is at least illuminating and perhaps startling to see, in this perspective, our usual assignment of studies in the freshman and sophomore years, our usual arrangements for classroom instruction and testing and examining, our usual social groupings of students in dormitories or fraternity houses or boardinghouses, our usual scheme of negative discipline. These are undoubtedly the best devices we have yet been able to construct. But in each of these fields, every teacher, at the least, dreams of something better. And the practical question is, Can we, under actual conditions, make our dreams come true; can we plan for something better and make our plans work? It is that question which the advisers faced as they entered upon their study of teaching method, of teaching content, and of determining conditions, for the lower college.

As we attempt to recount the discussions and the decisions of the advisers on these three specific questions, it is necessary to make our general principle, by one step, more specific. We have said that the lower college should prepare the young for the taking of personal responsibility. But it must do this in its own way and by the use of its own instruments. Its chosen material is literature; its chosen instrument is the book. The intention of the college is that, in the case of those favored young people who are allowed to study after the high-school period, minds shall be fed, and trained, and strengthened, and directed by the use of books. The whole procedure points forward to a mode of life in which persons, by the aid of books, are enabled to live in ways which are not open to their non-reading fellows, are trained to practice special forms of intelligence in which the use of books plays an essential part. And if this be true, then we have here the principle which must be used in all planning of the lower college.

In the discussion of proposals regarding methods, contents, or conditions of study, we must ask in every case, What effect will this arrangement have upon the eagerness and the capacity of a student to use books in the right way and for the right purposes? At the end of the two years our examination must be an attempt to discover how far the student has developed this attitude and this capacity. To put the matter sharply, we may say that the only really significant question to be asked concerning the graduate of a college as such is, Does he in his living depend upon books and does he use them effectively? Does he know what are the significant values, the significant problems, of his civilization; does he follow these as they are recounted and considered in news-

16

THE EXPERIMENTAL COLLEGE

Alexander Meiklejohn

The normal young American expects, and is led to expect, on his twenty-first birthday, not a new sense of responsibility, but a new automobile, a new set of opportunities for self-gratification. The Experimental College rests upon the assertion that against the specialized teaching of men for banking, for scholarship, for industry, for art, for medicine, and the like, there is the general liberal teaching of men for intelligence in the conduct of their own lives.

—ALEXANDER MEIKLEJOHN

"In the model created at Wisconsin, Alexander Meiklejohn shows what it means to have a genuine core curriculum. His ideas have both vitality and integrity."

—David Riesman
Harvard University
Author, *The Lonely Crowd*

"It is especially important to have Meiklejohn's guidance as we redefine liberal education for the modern world."

—Clark Kerr
President, Carnegie Council
on Higher Education

"We still need to think of bold and innovative experimentation in education. Meiklejohn helps show us the way."

—Wilber Cohen
Former Secretary of Health,
Education, and Welfare

SEVEN LOCKS PRESS
Cabin John, Md./Washington, D.C.

paper, in magazine, in books ranging from fiction to scholar-ly and technical discussion? Is he an intelligent reader?

In addition to the reading of books, practice in the arts and crafts and games can be used as an instrument of liberal education. For example, the activities of dramatics and dancing are at times startling in the richness of their contri-bution to the development of a student. And it is equally clear that both creative and receptive experiences in music, in painting, in sculpture, in architecture, in games—all these in significant and valuable ways play their parts in that enriching and strengthening of the human personality which we call liberal education.

II.

The Course of Study

CHAPTER FOUR

Understanding Is Integration

THE DEMAND FOR INTEGRATION is the demand that throughout a scheme of instruction there shall run a single and dominating "scheme of reference." It means that, logically considered, the course of study shall have unity, shall hang together from beginning to end. There shall not be a series of disconnected readings or separate topics whose relations are left undetermined. Fundamentally the course shall be the study of a single topic, and every separate subject within it shall be recognized as a special phase of the central inquiry. The effect of the principle is, it is obvious, the discarding of separate "subjects" as given in the usual college arrangements and the substituting for these of a single enterprise running through the two years of the course.

This demand for integration, for unification, of the curriculum has immediate regard to that quality which Mr. Flexner calls "intelligence, capable of being applied in any field whatever." The phrase suggests a mind which is able to go about, anywhere in the world of human experience, with sureness of footing, with certainty of touch. And the teaching question is, How does one develop and cultivate that quality in a growing, plastic mind? In answer to this question, the principle of integration, as discussed by the advisers, is very direct and simple in its teaching theory. It says that the student should go, in terms of ideas, into all the fields in which we wish him to be intelligent, that in each of these fields his mind should be given active work to do, and especially that these separate pieces of work should be such that they will run into one another, have intellectual relations with one another. The underlying purpose is that the student shall in this way develop a scheme of reference covering all the fields, within which each field shall find its proper place. And the result of this will be that any new experience within any field may then be seen in its place, in its relations, in the ways which we sum up under the terms, *with understanding* or *intelligently.* From this point of view the "intelligent" mind is not one which can go safely into unfamiliar fields. No mind can do that. Insofar as a field is unfamiliar, no thinking about it can be secure and certain. An intelligent mind is one to which, in some essential sense, all fields of experience are familiar.

As a boy seeks liberal education, as he comes out of the American school and the American home, as he enters upon the last formal stages of his training for self-direction, which will you stress more strongly, the gaining of specific information or the building up of a general scheme of reference? Now no single statement could summarize the varied responses of individual advisers to this question. In their decisions, however, one finds a general drift which may be defined by two statements. First, in the lower college years, under present teaching conditions, the "integration" demand is of primary importance. In the large, we may say that "information" is secondary; it is valuable, at this time and for these pupils, only as it contributes to the building up of one's scheme of reference. And second, there is at this point an important, though not radical, difference between the two years. Information about America is, for our teaching purpose, far more important than information about Athens. As a young man tries to bring into order the world of his values, beliefs, decisions, it makes very little difference, in the last resort, whether he knows what was going on in Athens twenty-four centuries ago. It is, however, essential that he know what is going on in the American world of today. Quite clearly the two years cannot then be simply subsumed under a blank generalization. They have a common aim, but they serve it in different ways. We must now try, by illustration, to make these statements more clear and perhaps more convincing.

In any organized understanding of contemporary life the distinction between riches and poverty must play an essential part. This cleavage in human societies is a vital element in any intelligent man's scheme of reference. How then shall we use studies in Athenian civilization of the fifth century B.C. for the teaching of freshman about it? Now the answer to that question depends upon our judgment as to what the ordinary American boy needs first to have done to his mind with respect to the problem of riches and poverty. And the answer of the scheme of reference view is that he needs, to begin with, not primarily more information but a more active response to the information which he already has.

If that response can be aroused, then one of its immediate effects will be a strenuous demand for further information. For example, every boy who comes to college knows in his own immediate circle of acquaintance the tragic separation between the rich and the poor. One pupil comes to the university with a credit in the bank of two or three thousand dollars. Another comes with two or three hundred dollars which he has earned during the summer. One is threatened by the dangers of wastefulness and folly. The other is uncertain whether or not he can "last the semester." Do they understand it? Do they regard it as something to be "understood," or do they simply accept it as matter of fact? If they do the latter they are, insofar, uneducated and failing in the essential process of getting an education. Now at this point we may use the experience of Athens for teaching purposes. Athens had always much to do with the problem of the rich and the poor. It is recorded that in one of the earlier centuries, as a result of changing social and external conditions which no one seemed to understand, the division between the two classes became desperately serious. The ownership of land was drifting into the hands of a few. More and more, the many were losing their freeholds, were becoming serfs, were selling their bodies to pay their debts. And as revolution threatened, all classes called upon Solon, who seemed both wise and honest, to take the city into his hands and to do with debts and ownership whatever he might think best. And so there came about the reforms of Solon. How shall this incident be used for teaching purposes?

It is clear that one might ask the student to learn, so far as he can, all that is known about the situation in Athens and about Solon's dealing with it. In very many excellent textbooks, this material has been gathered, and so arranged that it can be memorized even by the most inactive of minds. And it would be easy, too, for the teacher, in this case, to tell whether or not the pupil has done his learning faithfully and well. He can be tested and marked on his mastery of facts. But the trouble is that by assigning a task in this form we give to the student a wholly false suggestion as to what his mind should be doing. For a young American of eighteen or nineteen, in the present state of American society, to spend his powers in simply learning what was going on in the Athens of Solon would be an egregious waste of time, a sin against himself and against his approaching responsibilities.

The advisers have, therefore, with much misgiving and with many hesitations, contrived a different policy. They have said to the student, "Look into the situation with which Solon was dealing; put yourself into his place; try to imagine what was going on in his mind. Write a paper and tell what you would have done had you faced his responsibilities." And at this point there has occurred a curious reversal of teaching relationships. Having said to the students, "You must study Athens in order to understand America," we find ourselves constantly saying to them, "You must bring your knowledge of modern America to help you in interpreting ancient Athens."

When the freshmen were reading the Greek dramas we urged them to read also Ibsen and O'Neill; when they were studying Plato's *Republic*, we assigned the story of the Russian experiment in communism in Hindus's *Humanity Uprooted*. And the same procedure has been followed in matters of art, religion, politics, philosophy, and science.

And the belief underlying this method is very simple: Young Americans do not think about the information which they already have. We, too, have an economic and social crisis similar to that of Solon's time. With us, too, as a result of conditions which no one seems able to understand, the great bulk of the property tends to fall into the hands of a few; with us, too, the lower economic class is in terrible fear and distress; in America, as in Athens, unguided forces take from men their independence, make them the slaves of their fellows. And the primary task of liberal education is to make it impossible that students should be in such a situation without attempting to understand and control it.

The chief task of the teacher as he deals with American college students is to get their minds active, to give them a sense of the urgency of human need, to establish in them the activity of seeing and solving problems. It is true that they are sadly in need of information, but it is far more true that they need the desire for information. We must set them to work at a task where information is the basic material to be used. If they will attempt to build up a scheme of reference, then for them every new fact will take on significance, every new situation will become an object of active inquiry.

We have cited the division between the rich and the poor as one of the matters about which a lower college student should learn to think. Now, from the point of view of the principle of integration, the problem of devising a course of study is that of stating in orderly arrangement and inter-relation the essential problems with which human intelligence deals. One need hardly say that the advisers do not think themselves to have accomplished this task. What they can say is that, in their attempt to make and use a course of study, they have worked at the task and have tried to enlist their students in the same endeavor. Insofar as the college has been successful, both groups have been engaged in this never-accomplished but never-to-be-abandoned enterprise of the human spirit—the search for unified understanding.

As one goes through the records and other papers of the Experimental College, one finds there an indefinite number of attempts, made by many individuals, to organize the course of study in the terms suggested. No one of these has ever been formally adopted, and each has led to others which developed its tendency or which broke out against it in some other direction. It will perhaps serve the purposes of exposition if we give here an attempt made by the chairman of the college, in its third year, to formulate the principles on which the course of study was operating. A comparison of this statement with the assignments to the freshman and sophomore classes in the year 1930-31 will perhaps serve better than anything else to indicate the line of thought which the advisers had been following.*

It will be noted that the statement has all the roughness of a working document. It reads as follows:

Principles

1. The purpose of the course is to lead the student toward acquaintance with human intelligence as seen in two typical illustrations of its activity.

2. The term *intelligence* is interpreted as meaning all the creative activities, whether or not consciously directed, by which men strive to raise the quality of human experience.

3. It is assumed that in the two situations selected for study the same creative activities will appear, directed toward essentially the same ends under different conditions.

4. It is regarded as very important that the two years should be so dealt with as to form a single study (the attempt to see the human intelligence at work so that the student may be prepared to take his part in that work).

5. If we regard intelligence as the value response of the human individual to his situation, its activities may for purposes of study be classed into three groups.

   a. Activities immediately valuable in themselves—literature and the other arts, play, recreation, worship, enjoyment in all its forms. With respect to these the

---

*For freshman and sophomore class assignments, see Appendix II.

26

student should develop the power of critical appreciation.

b. The making and administering of social institutions—the arrangements by which groups of people provide for the furthering of common interests and the adjustment of conflicting interests. Matters to be studied here will present themselves as situations to be dealt with, the question being how, under actual conditions of human association, desirable ends can be achieved.

c. Intellectual activities which attempt to describe the world, as found in religion, science, and philosophy. In these activities individuals and groups are trying by the process of knowledge to determine what is the nature of themselves and of the surrounding "things" with which they have to deal; they seek an accounting of the forces available for the realizing of human purposes. In this field the student will face intellectual questions of fact and principle. For example, religious thinking asks whether human values have any place in the scheme of things at large. Science, assuming a time-space world, asks what things are and how they change. Philosophy asks the critical question, What is human intelligence and what is the world in relation to it?

6. As the student seeks acquaintance with the activities in these two situations and these three fields, it is essential that he become familiar with the best intelligence as found in a few of the greatest books. These books should be studied until they are known with genuine acquaintance.

CHAPTER FIVE

The Athens-America Curriculum

AT THE CLOSE of the year 1930-31, it was shrewdly suggested by one of the advisers that the college had already abandoned its original plan of studying and contrasting two civilizations. "We are now," he said, "studying not civilizations, but problems." The writer of this chapter does not accept that statement just as it stands. And yet it does seem to him to point to an important shift in both the theory and the practice of the college during its four years of experimentation. The shift in theory seems to be chiefly a clarification of an original idea which was at first vague and undetermined. The shift in practice is the seeking of new contents to serve a purpose now more adequately understood. The phrase "to study a civilization" has both changed and deepened in meaning as the advisers have used it. But whatever its form, there is no doubt that an important change has, in both parts of the course, taken place.

When the course was first announced, its avowed purpose was to study and contrast the Athens of Pericles with America in the nineteenth century. As the course is now given, the two human situations studied are, first, the Athens of Pericles and Plato and, second, modern, or even contemporary, America. In the freshman study, our scope has been enlarged to include the fourth as well as the fifth century. In the sophomore year, the contemporary situation has been added; we now explore not the nineteenth century exclusively, but modern America as a characteristic expression of human activity and intelligence.

In the original plan, as crudely conceived, there were

apparently four things which we wished the student to do during his two years. First, he was to become acquainted with Athens. Second, he was to become likewise acquainted with nineteenth-century America. And third, by comparing and contrasting these he was to make for himself an understanding of what a civilization is. But further, it should be noted, there was implied in these arrangements still another activity which was to come after the completion of the college course—that of taking this newly won insight into the life of twentieth-century America and using it there as an instrument of intelligent human living. Now the change which has come about in our interpretation of the plan has been that of perceiving more and more clearly that these are not, and should not be, four separate activities, carried on at four different times. One does not "learn" Athens, and then "learn" America, and then "learn" to compare them, and then "learn" how to live in terms of this wisdom. One of the most striking—and to some of our friends, the most shocking—illustrations of this point is that in the studies of the second year there have been practically no explicit comparisons made between the Athens of the first year and the America of the second. Apparently we have studied America as if we had never heard of Athens at all. In that statement, perhaps more clearly than in any other way, is revealed the inherent logic of the decisions which the advisers have been making.

Of the statement just made, two explanations may be given, each of which is, so far as it goes, true. One of them is negative and perhaps unsympathetic. The other is positive and seems to us to constitute a genuine justification of the procedure followed. The negative explanation is that the first year's study of Athens has not given to the students enough accurate and detailed and remembered information to serve as a useful basis of comparison with America. In large measure this statement is true.* But probably more impor-

---

*It is worthy of note, then, that in all the "information" tests taken, the students of the college have been surprisingly successful, in comparison with other student groups.

tant is the fact that, even if the students had been sufficiently well informed to make the comparison suggested, the teachers in the second year would not have been equipped to help them in the operation. Now these protestations of relative ignorance are not made with the intention of asserting that lack of information about Athens or about any other civilization is a virtue. In itself, such ignorance is undesirable and even deplorable. But the simple fact is—and here we come to the positive and more sympathetic interpretation—that the securing of detailed and remembered information about Athens has seemed to us quite secondary in relation to a more important purpose which the study of that civilization can serve. That purpose, it need hardly be said, is the fashioning of a scheme of reference which a student may bring to his study of later civilizations.

The statement in this form brings us back to our first query—have we then abandoned the study of Athens as a civilization? And the answer is, "No." We have studied it in the way which our purpose of liberal teaching requires. We have seen it not merely as a set of specific facts, but as typical, as representative, as significant for anyone who is trying to understand human living. And here we find the essential point. From the beginning of the first year, the student must be carrying on the "fourth" operation in the previously given list. His attempt at "understanding" must not wait until he has learned enough facts to serve as its basis. It must be present at the first and throughout the process, as the motivating purpose of all his studying. We should not send our students into a human situation as tourists go to a foreign country—with a list of important items to see and check. They should go rather as residents, for a time, sharing, so far as they can, in the life and experience of the people—getting the feel and the sense of their scheme of living. In the latter case they may have little to tell when they return, but they may perhaps be more reasonable and intelligent in their attitudes toward "foreign" people.

What, then, is the function of the Athenian year as we

have used it in our scheme of study? We have assumed that the student's purpose in studying a foreign civilization is to do with regard to it what any intelligent person living within that civilization would be trying to do—to see it in some such ordered way as that suggested in the last chapter. To understand a civilization is nothing else than to face and to solve, so far as one can, the questions with which its intelligence is dealing. It is chiefly because the literature of Athens is peculiarly well adapted to serve as the basis for an attempt at ordered thinking that we have chosen it as the subject matter of the first year. Other minds have excelled the Athenian in the breadth and scope of acquired knowledge, but at least so far as the remaining literature reveals, no other mind has equaled it in the liveliness, the determination, the precision of its effort to "make sense" out of the human enterprise, to understand what men are and what they are doing—in a word, to be liberally educated. To many of us it seems clear that for a young man beginning to put into form his scheme of reference, no other civilization could be so illuminating.

What then, again, is the change which has taken place in the course of study? In the freshman year we began with Pericles; we then moved on to include Plato. Our first thought had been that the student should see the Great Age as a set of objective achievements. But later it became clear that for us the significance, the meaning, of those achievements is not to be found in them, as such, as in the writing about them by men such as Plato and Thucydides. We must read the dramatists who came before and with and after Pericles; we must read Thucydides, who tells the tragic story of the rise of the city under its leader and of its decline in later years; and especially we must read Plato, who, seeing both the glory and the tragedy, tries to think it all through as a scheme of life, to discover its meaning, to plan for its more genuine and permanent success. The shift in the freshman year has come from the perception that what we wish our students to get is not primarily an acquaintance with the Greek situation, but an acquaintance with the

Greek mind, a sense of Greek intelligence at work upon its situation.

And the change in the sophomore teaching is another aspect of the same drift. In the original notion, the sophomore year was to be, like the freshman, preparatory. The student, having seen one civilization far in time and circumstance from the present, was to study another, near to the present, so that by the comparison and contrast of these two he might then move on to the interpretation of his own present world. But in the sophomore year as now conceived, preparation is over; the student is at work upon his final and permanent intellectual task. This is the last year of his formal liberal training. The time has come for him to ask for and to take self-direction in an actual world. He must, therefore, now study the modern, the American, mind at work upon the situation in the midst of which he is to live. He must share in the thinking which is now being done or, perhaps better, in that which ought to be done. He must show himself ready to assume intellectual responsibilities. Here, too, one finds the explanation of the greater emphasis in the second year on the acquiring and keeping of significant information. In order that a student may understand the problems of his own time and place, it is not enough that he formulate those problems in general terms which are applicable to all civilizations. He must also see them as they are set and modified by the peculiarities of value and of circumstance which determine in the present age and country the special issues with which it must deal. Human problems must now become local and contemporary and specific issues. And as he grapples with these, the student will face the necessity of knowing what the sciences of the modern world are doing, what are the current and developing processes of industry and commerce, how the agencies of government operate and change, how the activities of modern men come into being, are built up or torn down, are hindered or enhanced, what is going on in the fields of art, literature, play, religion, philosophy. About all these, as they are actually going on, the student must learn to read intelligently. It is the purpose of the sophomore year to try to get him firmly on his feet in that activity.

As already suggested, it would be quite hopeless to record here the detailed working out of the course of study which has been built upon the basis just described. It may, however, be worthwhile to read the topics assigned for papers to be written by the students. These perhaps better than anything else will indicate the intent of the advisers as they have tried to direct and influence the minds of their pupils.*

If one could see the assignments in relation to (1) the talks and lectures in which the reading and topics are discussed, and (2) the conferences between adviser and pupil before and after the paper is done, one would appreciate the course of study as it has been in action.

---

*For freshman and sophomore class assignments, see Appendix II.

CHAPTER SIX

Comments

IN THE PRECEDING chapters we have described the course of study as directed toward the making and using of a scheme of reference. It has already been noted that no such scheme has ever been formally adopted by the advisers. Far more important, however, is the fact that such formulations as we have made have not been presented to the students. Nothing could have been further from our intention than that the students should "learn" such a scheme from us, that they should be told in the abstract what are the essential problems of any civilization, and that they should then go forth, as it were with memory in hand, to look for the problems which have been listed. Success in the initiating of students into the art of thinking does not consist in getting them to learn a list of the questions which intelligent men ask. At this point, progress in the art which makes intelligence is not different from that in any other art. Rules and precepts should emerge as incidents in the course of practice. What one would expect to find in a well-trained intelligence is not primarily a set of remembered formulas, but a kind of intellectual sensitiveness, an ability to use one's eyes when a situation is presented, to use one's mind when its nature or its interests are to be considered, to act sensibly when action is needed. In a word, training in liberal thinking is not the giving of a scheme of reference to be remembered; it is the stimulating of a mind to make a scheme of reference for its own use. The present chapter will describe several specific features of the teaching plan as dominated by this principle.

1. The Regional Study

In June of the freshman year, as they come to the end of their study of Athens, the freshmen are asked to select for like study an American community. It is understood that through the summer vacation, so far as possible, and until the end of the first semester of the next year, they will gather all available information about this community and will write an account of it as an episode in human civilization. The task is, or should be, present to their minds over a period of seven or eight months. In general, a student selects the village or county or town or city in which he has lived. His problem is then to see with new eyes and to think with new thoughts an old and familiar situation. By way of preparation for this work the students are expected to read *Middletown* and to look over other surveys of American and foreign communities. What form the study shall take depends of course very largely upon the size and situation and surroundings of the community. The young man who studies a village with only three or four hundred inhabitants will probably find little literature, scanty statistics, slight historical records dealing with his material. He can, however, study the region as a place of human habitation, can find out why people came there and have remained, what activities were open to them, what use they have made of their opportunities in terms of climate, soil, power, and other determining factors; he can trace the developments of their group life in terms of education, religion, amusement, cultural interests of various sorts. And as he thus tries to understand and appreciate the life of a community, he must, of course, seek information and insight wherever he can find it. In the small village he will talk with his parents, with the minister, the keeper of town or county records, the librarian and school principal, the antiquarian, the leading merchants, the teller of town stories. And he is expected to gather together all this material and to think and write it into a significant account of the life and experience of the place. If a student selects a large city for study, his problem is very different. Usually here he is overwhelmed with records but scantily supplied with personal impressions. Very commonly, within the larger picture of the life of a city he must select some special region or special phase for study. In several cases two or more students have in this way worked together on the same community. By special arrangement in the year 1931-32, a group of six students are joining forces in a study of Madison where, with immediate access to their material, they will be able constantly to check their work by personal observations. But however the work is done, we have found it one of the most valuable of educational devices. When it was given to the first class, a very large number of them shrank from it as something of which they were wholly incapable. Now, however, it has become an accepted part of the routine, and very many of the students pursue it with keen delight. As a part of the program it has the effect of adding to the two situations studied, Athens and America, a third episode which has the liveliness of interest of immediate and concrete experience.

2. Examinations

For two reasons examinations have entered into the program of the Experimental College. In the first place, the fact that our graduates must take their places in the junior class as candidates for degrees has made it necessary that we grade them, recommend their promotion or the denial of it, determine the value of their credits in the usual terms of grade points. But also, quite apart from this necessity, the estimating of the quality of a student's achievement at the end of his course seems in itself important and desirable. As a basis for further planning of his career, a student should be told what his teachers think of the work which he has already done. But what form shall the examining take? Nothing is more revealing of the purpose underlying a course of study than the nature of the examinations given at its close. Nothing is more effective in telling the student what we want him to do than the method we take of finding out whether or not, and how well, he has done it. As forms of communication between faculty and students, examinations may do much good, but they are also capable of doing incalculable harm. Their very common suggestion that a "subject" has now been learned, that the student may now be certified as having "taken" and "passed" a course, is perhaps the most destructive single influence which our educational machinery has produced.

In December 1928, the advisers, after long discussion, adopted the following vote upon the grading of students at the end of the two-year course:

That the grading shall be determined entirely upon the basis of the quality of three pieces of work: (a) the Regional Study, (b) a special study made by a student in the third term upon a topic chosen by him from a list prepared by the advisers, and (c) a general objective test on material not specifically related to the course of study in the Experimental College.

Notes:

1. It is understood that this proposal does not preclude arrangement for outside examiners to share in or to take charge of the estimating of the quality of the three pieces of work specified.

2. It is understood that oral examining may be used in determining the quality of any piece of work.

3. It is understood that in cases where the estimating of the quality of the student's work is difficult, the examiners may turn for assistance to the impressions of the student recorded by his advisers during the course of his two years in the college.

On the negative side, this legislation excluded two kinds of grading. It provides that none of the regular work of the college, except the Regional Study and the long paper written in the last semester, shall be considered in the fixing of the final grade. Throughout the two years teacher and pupil associate together with no sense that one is "marking" the other. And, second, so far as the final mark is concerned, no attempt is made to see how much of the material studied the student remembers. Tests of memory are at times given for teaching purposes but not for the determining of grades. So much for negations! On the positive side, the arrangement means that the advisers wish to know what, under normal conditions of work, a student is able to do with the sort of task for which education is preparing him. The question is not, "What has he done in the past?" but, "What can he do now?" In terms of our working principle we may well ask, Can he study an American community and give an intelligent account of its situation and its experience? Can he read a great book in which one of the best of American minds is discussing our external achievements and our inner life? If a student is able to do these things properly by the use of materials which are available to anyone who normally attempts such a task, then we need not stop to inquire how much he recalls of what he has heard or read. We have been trying to get him ready for a certain kind of intelligent endeavor. Our examination question is therefore, "Can he successfully carry on such an endeavor?" In this, as in many another case, the proof of the pudding may be found, not in the examining of the kitchen machinery, but, in the eating of the pudding itself.

Two points should be noted in passing. First, in actual operation practically no stress has been laid upon the "objective test" referred to as one of the bases of grading. And second, in the last two years the final paper has dealt with *The Education of Henry Adams* rather than with a special topic chosen by the student himself. Upon the quality of this paper and of the Regional Study, the final marks have been given.

3. The Teaching of Science

As one runs through the records and notes of the advisers' meetings, one finds a curious succession of educational discussions. At one meeting men from many different departments are considering how economic problems shall be presented and studied. Soon after, the same men are dealing with political situations, and then, it may be, with geographical influences; later, perhaps, they must decide upon the selection of literature, the principles of architecture, the conditions of city planning; at some other period, religion, philosophy, or physics demands their attention and decision. Though their special interests and training are in different fields, they must nevertheless think together and decide together upon all the varied aspects of the year's curriculum. In every such discussion one will, of course, find the man in whose field the special topic lies taking the lead, the primary responsibility, and yet it can be fairly said that group thinking has been carried on and that common decisions have been made upon the course of study. At very considerable cost in distraction and strain, the advisers, at least, have been going through a lively process of liberal education.

Now it would be hopeless to attempt to give in this report an account of all the problems met and the decisions made in the attempt at teaching the different phases of Greek and American civilization. For our present purpose it must suffice to give as illustration a brief account of arrangements made for the teaching of science.

The contribution of science to human civilization must be a major, a dominating element in any study of modern civilization. What science means in terms of human insight into the world, in terms of human mastery over fate, no one as yet knows. But whatever the ultimate judgment upon it, there can be no doubt that the scientific attitude and method is now, more than any other single influence, in command of the modern world. It is essential, therefore, that students who are being trained for human responsibility should know, so far as they can, what it is and what it does.

The first plan of the advisers was made along lines of physiology. One of our number was a worker in that field, and he devised for us a combination of laboratory work and reading which seemed very promising. The plan was, however, given up because of difficulties and expense involved in securing proper equipment and assistance. The second attempt has been made chiefly, though not wholly, in the direction of the physical sciences. The following selection from a memorandum prepared by Mr. Havighurst will indicate its general direction.

SECOND-YEAR SCIENCE
IN THE EXPERIMENTAL COLLEGE

Purpose of the Science Study

When we attempted to organize our study of modern science so that it might contribute to our general aim of helping the student to understand himself and his world, we set up the following three goals:

1. The student should become acquainted with the modern scientific world-picture, and he should learn the difference between it and other world-pictures, present and past, scientific and nonscientific.

2. The student should be helped toward an understanding of modern science which includes a critical understanding of the validity of its world-picture and an appreciation of the possibilities and limitations of its methods.

3. The student should learn enough of modern science to see that it has created the material basis of modern civilization.

To reach these goals our study must depend upon *interpretation* of the facts of science as well as upon a knowledge of the facts themselves. We must somehow effect a compromise between the learning of facts and the interpretation of these facts. No matter how limited the time (and our time for the study of modern science is limited to a little less than one-fourth of the sophomore year), it must be shared between facts and interpretation.

We are not attempting to prepare our students for

40

technical work in science. Most of them will never study science again in a formal way. They will have no practical use for the scientific facts which they learn. A knowledge of scientific facts is necessary to them only as an aid to their understanding of the meaning of science in modern life. Hence we have tried to make our factual study of science keep step with our attempts at interpretation of science.

Undoubtedly our students cannot pass a fact test in science as well as college students who have had the usual one-year elementary course in physics or chemistry or biology. On the other hand, our students are far superior to these others in their understanding of the meaning of science.

If we have leaned too far in one direction, it has probably been in the direction of interpretation. I think that in 1928-29, our first year of sophomore work, when our students spent no time in the laboratory, we did pay too little attention to the facts of science. Since that time, I believe that we have struck a better working balance between facts and interpretation.

Plan of Study

During the last three years we have devoted the first eight weeks of the sophomore year to the study of physics and biology. We use these terms in a broad sense—physics includes some astronomy and chemistry while biology includes some physiology and psychology. The time we devote to science in the second year is the equivalent of about seven semester hours as calculated on the ordinary basis of fifteen semester hours to a full semester's work.

Laboratory Work

The work in physical science includes laboratory work in physics. This is the only laboratory work that we do, and it is done in physics rather than biology mainly for the reason that such an arrangement was the most practicable one in our situation. Each student is given the opportunity to spend five two-hour periods a week for one month in the physics laboratory.

Work in Physics

In addition to the laboratory work, we have four or five lecture or discussion periods a week. Some of these periods are devoted to demonstration of experiments which the students cannot perform. But most of these meetings are given to discussion of the work in the laboratory or of the reading assignments.

Instead of a textbook of the usual sort, we use a text which has been prepared especially for this work. This text contains an outline of the material to be covered, directions for the experimental work, and some discussion of the interpretation of the facts of physical science. Students are expected to go to regular elementary physics textbooks (which we provide) for detailed explanations of the particular subjects on which they work in the laboratory. Students are also expected to do some general reading on the world-picture of physical science, and the advisers suggest to them books which are adapted to their individual preparations and abilities. The better students are advised to read Jeans's *Universe Around Us*, while those who are not so well prepared are sent to more elementary books like W. H. Bragg's *Concerning the Nature of Things*.

As the close of the work in physical science, one or two weeks have been given to reading and discussion in biological science, concentrating on the idea of evolution. In 1931-32, all the students read G. H. Parker, *What Evolution Is*, while the majority also read sections of Baitsell, *Evolution of Earth and Man*, and other books on evolution.

No one who has had touch with this venture in the teaching of science can hold the opinion that the venture has been carried through to a successful ending. There is still a long road to travel before that can be said. We are not certain about the use of the laboratory or of mathematics, and, in a field which grows by leaps and bounds, the choice of books cannot possibly be fixed. On the other hand, we are all convinced that there is, at this point, one of the most vital problems of modern education for which the regular teaching of science and related subjects does not make adequate provision. For example, the students who come to us after many years of study in mathematics have, on the whole, no conception of mathematics as an instrument of scientific investigation, no facility in its use in relation to its primary purpose. Mathematics has been "done," but it has been neither understood nor used. We need from the schools a quite different training from that which they have given. And the same seems to us largely true of the usual separate course in science given in the separate departments. They do not adequately serve the purposes of nonscientists who need, for the sake of general intelligence, to "read" science just as they read political or philosophical or literary discussions.

4. Major Books

When the dominating ideas and purpose of a course of study have been accepted, the problem becomes largely that of finding books which will express the idea and serve the purpose. And from the very beginning it has been taken for granted by the advisers that, just so far as possible, the books selected should be "great," should represent the work of the human mind in its highest quality as well as in relation to its most significant themes. We are certain that one of the greatest educational influences is found in this closeness of contact with the leaders in human intelligence. Teaching rests largely in the hope that greatness of mind may be contagious.

In the development of the curriculum toward its present form, two major books have come to take a primary place, one in relation to each civilization. The Greek studies have been largely centered round the *Republic* of Plato, together with a number of the related Dialogues. In the American assignments, *The Education of Henry Adams* has, in some measure, taken a corresponding place. In the first of these two cases, it is clear that by other groups of teachers other choices might have been made. It would have been quite possible to take Thucydides as the basis with his keen and accurate historical studies. The four great dramatists have often been used, and might well be used again, as giving approach to Greek life and thought. It is quite possible that the architecture, sculpture, and related arts and crafts might be used for the purpose with telling effect. Each of these has been used in its own field. On the whole, however, Plato has seemed to us best suited to give center and focus to the scheme of teaching. We have hoped that by constant and recurring contacts the freshmen might catch something of his scheme of reference, something of his far-reaching insight, his deep and passionate human spirit.

The choice of *The Education of Henry Adams* for the second year has been made with less assurance. It is a very difficult book for sophomores as well as a very significant one. Some of the advisers question whether its influence contributes strongly toward the building up of intellectual and moral power in relation to the problems of American life. They fear that students may be baffled and defeated by it. But on the other side is the conviction that in the book one finds a very powerful and sophisticated mind, thoroughly at home in the processes of American civilization, finding itself thwarted and defeated only because it goes out to meet every actual shock and to face every real problem. It is possible that if another book of like ''greatness'' could be found to challenge the *Education*, a substitution might be made. But thus far the advisers have been unsuccessful in their search. There can be no doubt that if a student does succeed in mastering the book, he has made a long step forward in the process of his education.

5. Training in Writing

It is worthy of note that throughout the two years the course of study provides that students have practice and criticism in writing. Every week during the two years papers are submitted in rough draft or in final form to an adviser, and out of his own nontechnical experience the adviser gives such assistance as he can. The influence toward ready and good writing is informal, but it is steady and apparently powerful.

6. Independent Reading

It may be noted also that an effect of the course of study, as devised and used, is to stimulate free reading in important books. Many of the students have built up relatively large private libraries. A very large proportion of them have developed the taste and the habit of free, independent enjoyment of significant reading.

7. Foreign Language

Instruction in foreign languages has been given chiefly in extra courses taken "on the Hill." When the college opened, it was hoped that this work might be woven into the teaching of the two civilizations. However, administrative difficulties and lack of time have prevented thus far the realization of this hope. It is worthy of note in passing that a voluntary class in Greek, in which usually from ten to fifteen students were enrolled, has been extraordinarily successful.

III.

The Methods
of Teaching

CHAPTER SEVEN

The Individual Student
and His Freedom

WE HAVE SEEN our working principle express itself in the course of study in the demand for a *required* curriculum. A college, we have said, is a group of teachers and pupils, all of whom are reading the same books, trying to solve the same problems. No one who is not reading those books, working on those problems, is a member of that college. In the very nature of the case, the purpose and the materials of a liberal college define a common curriculum.

Now it is a curious fact that this same working principle, when applied to methods of teaching, expresses itself not in requirement, but in freedom of action. When a young man comes to that stage in his education in which it is to be determined whether or not he is capable of free and responsible self-direction, the use of any other methods than those of freedom is a contradiction in terms. It would be arrant nonsense to graduate a student from the lower college with the statement, "This fellow is capable of directing his own life if someone else will direct him how to do it." Before we can guarantee him as ready for mature living, we must have evidence of his own capacity and fitness, his own maturity of judgment and attitude. And from this it follows that our relationship with him, during these two decisive years, must be one in which, to the utmost possible limit, he is given his freedom of action, is allowed to choose his own way of life. As we try to develop the meaning of this statement, two preliminary remarks must be made.

First, the argument here presented is not merely

dialectical. It springs from hard experience which comes to every teacher of college students. It is an observation based on bitterly won common sense. We wish our students to reach a certain level of intelligent self-direction. How shall that end be achieved? What can we do to bring it about? Shall we force the student into a sense of responsibility? Shall we drive him into freedom? We would gladly use these methods if they were effective. In fact, we would go even further than that. So valuable are freedom and self-direction that if only some physician would invent a serum which, upon injection, would produce in a student those qualities, we would willingly substitute for the classroom the operating table, would joyfully assume the roles of nurse and orderly in place of that of pedagogue. But the plain fact is that no such specific has yet been discovered. And it is equally clear that the methods of inducement and compulsion do not give us the desired result. You can train a student for freedom only by building up more and more his freedom in all your relationships with him.

And second, the suggestion that a student should be made free by his teachers does not mean, as it is often assumed to mean, that the teacher has nothing to do for the pupil. It is a caricature of the suggestion to say, "The teacher presents the course of study; the student accepts or rejects it according to his own sweet will; and that is the sum of the whole matter." Giving people freedom is not so simple, so negative a program as that. Throughout the history of mankind, the experience of every democratic enterprise reveals the fact that the attempt to deal with men and women, not by compulsion, but by regarding them as free and equal with their fellows, is an amazingly difficult and complicated undertaking. Far from saying that during the two years of the lower college the teacher has nothing to do for his pupil, this suggestion implies that at no other point in the educational scheme is the influence of the teacher so vitally important, so tragically decisive of the future character and destiny of the student. Teachers in the lower college are commissioned by society to convey a message to young men between the ages of eighteen and twenty. They are not saying, "Do as you please." Rather, they are saying, "The time has come for your freedom; no one else can give it to you; you must, therefore, make it for yourself." And the question of teaching method is, How can that message be delivered effectively?

Now this situation, as one meets it in the lower college, is in outline a very simple one. A young American comes to us for instruction. We wish him to adopt a certain mode of living—that of seeking intelligence by means of books. But the suggestion does not apparently attract him. He has been formed and shaped by a society which does not regard living in the companionship of books as constituting great success or high achievement. How, then, shall we counteract the effects of other training; how shall we influence the pupil to go in the right direction? It is obvious that the question here involved is one of motives—that is, of forces available within the personality of the pupil which may be used for the accomplishing of a desired end. What, then, are the "motives" on which a teacher may depend as he plans his scheme of education? First, of course, is the direct appeal of approaching responsibilities. The teacher may say, "There are things to be done in American life, in your life; you must be ready to do them. And further, in the doing of those things, some men, at least, must be users of books. Are you ready to be one of them? Will you make yourself ready? Can we count on you to become an intellectually equipped member of American society?" There can be no doubt that this is the primary appeal which every teacher uses; it is, and must be, the basis of the scheme of teaching. But it is at least possible that this direct approach may not be effective. It may ring in the ears of the students and still leave them sitting idly on the benches. Are there not, then, other auxiliary, secondary motives which may be used? Anyone who is acquainted with students knows that there are. They fall into three groups.

First, if a student has not the zest for learning, we may still prod him into the use of books by appeal to his other desires and to the fears which grow out of these. For example, we may say to the young man who sits idly on the bench, "If you do not do your lessons, you will not be allowed to join a fraternity; you will be forbidden to play on the football team; you will be 'dropped' from college and sent home in disgrace; you will be required to attend classes when better students are allowed to be absent." Just as we lure a child into the taking of bitter medicine by the promise of sugar candy to follow, so we may entice the young man of eighteen into the doing of the hated task by the prospect of joys or the fear of miseries to come. And second, in the case of abler students, at least, there is the very effective appeal to vanity. Students may be stirred to special activity and industry by the arrangement that if their achievement in the classroom is superior to those of their fellows, this fact will be publicly announced. They will be recognized, by means of prizes and honors, as more clever, more successful than other students. They will be given opportunity to find satisfaction in their own superiority. And third, much wider in the range of its application is the desire for social approval, the instinct of social conformity. We may convince students that, whatever the merits or lack of merit of the educational enterprise, sober and respectable people think well of those who achieve formal success in it and think badly of those who fail. And this being true, we can, by the establishing of a general scheme of "grading," bring upon the whole body of students a social pressure of very great weight. The desire to "make good" is a factor that can be counted on in the management of any American enterprise.

And now, with this array of motive forces at his disposal, what shall the procedure of the teacher be? The answer of the advisers, so far as it is revealed in their practice, can be stated in very simple terms. It is that, to the utmost possible limit, the secondary forces should be eliminated from the teaching process; that, just so far as it can be done, the stress of emphasis should be placed upon the direct appeal of the work itself which the student ought to be doing. We should give to students a free and unhindered opportunity to decide whether or not they wish to be educated men. And nothing else should be allowed to confuse, or to distract attention from, that decision.

That the secondary methods do confuse the issue seems beyond question. This can be shown in each of the cases mentioned. We can, by the use of external rewards and penalties, induce unwilling students to use books. But what, in the process, do books become for the student? What is the meaning of education for him? The effect is to make of learning a disagreeable task which, so long as one is under the control of teachers, must be performed for the sake of other values. And from this it follows, that, after the pressure is removed, all motive force for the using of books disappears with it. It is well for us to remember that the graduates of American colleges are not peculiarly marked by their ardent devotion to good reading. And in the same way, the appeal to vanity defeats its own intention. Insofar as a scheme of education leads a person to rejoice in his own cleverness, his own superiority, it is bad education. Insofar as it tends to substitute for the genuine appeal of objective interest, this form of self-seeking is positively disastrous. And the same is true of the appeal to social conformity. This is a motive which has no place in the education of a young person whose present task it is to criticize, to appraise, to challenge conventional standards and valuations. At the time when he is learning to stand on his own feet we must not ask him to find strength and support in the general, uncriticized judgments of his fellows. To do so is to defeat both him and ourselves. There is nothing for it but to keep his mind, so far as we can, on the thing which he is doing as worthy of doing for its own sake.

In this connection it may be worthwhile to note two classes of students whom one finds peculiarly difficult to deal with for purposes of liberal education. The first is the boy who has developed a special interest and has discovered in himself special aptitude for it. He can "write" or "act" or "do mathematics." And because he can do this thing well he wishes to devote himself to it. And then, out of the desire and perhaps out of the encouragement given him by others, there springs the conviction that for him proper education lies along the line of this study in which he is successful. He becomes a victim of the "bias of happy exercise." To such students it is often practically impossible to present the values of being intelligent. They have confused scholarship with intelligence. The second class of difficult cases is found among the conventionally "good students." These have learned their lessons well because they are pliable in disposition, are willing and eager to do whatever their parents, their teachers, the general social scheme may ask of them. As one faces such students, the feeling of futility sometimes rises to sheer desperation. They are so willing to do what you ask because you ask it. And what you wish as a teacher is that they should see for themselves the human necessity which underlies all lessons, should feel its drive and compulsion, should undertake their own education. Here again the motive force is wholly self-denying and self-defeating. One cannot be dependent in being independent. There is a certain sense in which every good student must become a bad one before his goodness can become his own.

On the basis of what has been said, it is now possible to state the basic working principle of the advisers with regard to method of teaching. We shall find it appearing in both negative and positive forms.

Negatively, the principle rests in the conviction that the failure of the enterprise of learning to catch the imagination, to move the will of young America, is largely due to confusion caused by the use of the secondary motives to which we have referred. Young men are not excited about learning because they have been made, by compulsions and inducements of various sorts, to think of it as something quite different from what it is. On the negative side, therefore, the advisers have gone to the limit in excluding such devices from their procedure. Except at two points at which obligations to the university regime rendered special arrangements necessary, no regulations have been made, attendance has not been taken, penalties have not been inflicted, inducements have not been offered, grades have not been given. We have assumed that the most effective way of presenting to students the opportunities and the obligations of self-direction is to give them in their own student experience those obligations and opportunities. We have persistently refused to take upon ourselves responsibilities which, if they are fulfilling the intent of the college, are theirs. We have tried to keep the issue of intelligence in action as clear and direct as possible.

But now, with the field thus negatively cleared, what is the positive program? How shall book-intelligence be so presented that it shall be effective upon the habits and minds of our pupils? It is clear that, in the teaching situation, there are two forms of personal influence on which we can rely—that of the teacher and that of the college community within which the student lives. First then, we may so arrange relations between teacher and pupil that the personal attitude of the former shall have a chance to communicate itself to the latter. And second, we may so construct our community life that books and the use of them shall be at home in it, shall be the natural focus of its enthusiasms and purposes. Teaching arrangements and community living—these two must be established on the supposition that they are the friendly activities of a group of older and younger students. The elaboration of this statement, so far as it refers to the making of the community, must be left for a later section of this report. For the present our interest is in its significance for the forming of teaching relationships.

In the field of teaching method it has seemed to us that, in order to present effectively to the student the enterprise of intelligence, we must deal with him primarily as an individual. We must substitute for the scheme of instruction which is based upon the classroom a scheme which rests primarily upon personal conference. As American students now come to the college, it seems evident that the most effective way to enlist their activity in the cause of the college is to deal with each student separately, to get acquainted with him as he is, with all his peculiarities of power and of limitation; to bring him into informal contact with an older person who, having gone through the undergraduate stage, is now engaged in the activities which we wish the student to follow; to let these two talk together in relations of free and untrammeled conversation. We have, therefore, taken the "personal conference," not, it is true, as a total teaching scheme, but as the basis of a scheme, as expressing more adequately than anything else the purpose which we have in mind and the method which we intend to follow.

The next two chapters will try to give in some detail the working out of a teaching program on the basis just stated. Before that is done, however, several explanatory remarks are in order.

First, the adoption of the principle of freedom in dealing with students, the abolition of external complusions and rewards, does not mean that the work of the student is not to be judged and criticized, approved and condemned. Quite the contrary is the case. It is true that we have taken it as a primary principle that in the personal conference no marks shall be given, no grades shall be reported to someone else. It has seemd to us essential that the meeting of teacher and pupil be wholly freed from that external influence. But, nevertheless, the essential quality of the relationship is one of criticism. The student, as such, is engaged in doing a piece of work; special phases of that work have been from time to time assigned; he brings to his adviser his results. And the primary purpose is that the adviser should help him to see the merits and defects of what he has done. The teacher is attempting to introduce his apprentice into the mysteries of the craft of learning. He must, therefore, make him aware of the quality of what he has already done, must give him a growing appreciation of the skill and mastery which are still to be achieved. Teaching by personal conference is a peculiar combination of personal friendliness and candid, impersonal criticism.

And second, the method of freedom does not mean that appeal is made, solely or even primarily, to the interest of the student. The teacher's question to the student is not, "Do you find this interesting?" but rather, "Do you see why this is important and significant?" And if a matter is important, then it makes no difference whether or not the student has a taste, a liking, for it. If there is some human situation which needs to be understood in order that a young man may live intelligently, then he should go vigorously about it, just as a would-be football player spends weary and painful hours in tackling a dummy or building up the muscles in his legs and back. There is, of course, a principle of limitation at this point. Not all young men can be made good football players; and the severity of training toward the end of the season is quite different from that which is given when the new recruits make their first appearance on the field. But in spite of the limitation, the fact remains that the primary appeal of all liberal teaching is not to a student's interests taken as separate things, but to a judgment of value and worthfulness made by him as a responsible human being.

The statement just made needs, if not correction, at least supplementation by another which appears to be in conflict with it. This is the assertion that the teacher must have constant regard for the interest and peculiar capacities of his pupils. These interests are the active forces in the pupil's make-up. As such they are himself; they are the materials which the teacher must use. Just as one cannot make a silk purse out of a sow's ear, so one cannot make a student except as activities already stirring within him can be taken and transformed into the ways of learning. Each student then presents a different teaching problem. Each must be treated differently. Each must go a different way toward the common goal. Each must start at the task where he is and must work where and how his nature requires. And the teacher must accept these differences and deal with his varying students accordingly. There can be no doubt that, as a description of teaching method, these assertions are true. And yet they do not mean that the teacher accepts the interests of his students as determining the aim of his teaching. They are not the aim, the goal, of teaching; they are the materials to be used in reaching a goal which is set by nothing less than all the interests for which a human being should have regard, whether he has them now or not. In a word, each student must, in the nature of the case, go his own way. If he does not walk on his own legs, he will not walk at all. But if he goes rightly, he goes toward the meeting of an obligation which is common to every human being, teacher and pupil, nonteacher and nonpupil alike. To teach him is to get him to assume freely his responsibilities.

CHAPTER EIGHT

The Principle at Work

WE HAVE TWO YEARS in which to train young men in the art of reading for intelligence: How shall it be done? It is evident that the plan of teaching must be devised with two ends in view. First, we must develop the student's intention, his purpose to read; and second, we must build up his capacity, his ability to read well. The teaching aim has to do both with the will and with the mind. There are, therefore, two measures of success in teaching, and, correspondingly, two measures of failure. If a student leaves us with capacity for learning but with no active interest in the using of that capacity, we have in the latter respect failed. If he goes out eager for knowledge but is dull, inaccurate, and ill-equipped in mental technique, we have again fallen short of our proper achievement. The two aims, the two characters at which we aim, are of course interdependent. Out of the eager pursuit of learning comes improvement in the quality of learning. And one of the strongest incentives to learning, as to any other activity, is the sense of doing it well. And yet the two are not identical. Any practical teaching scheme must have regard for these as separate ends and, according to the peculiarities of varying student nature, must adjust its emphasis to the needs of the pupil concerned.

Now in dealing with the general run of students who enter an American college, it is important to remember that the active forces within and around them are not driving them on into the eager pursuit of liberal learning. The American home, the American school, the American social order, do not, at present, create acceptance of the values of liberal understanding. They implant many other desirable and attractive qualities, but not that. And from this it follows that, in the great majority of cases, our primary task as teachers is not the cultivation of excellence, but the arousing of activity. We are trying to get an enterprise started, rather than to carry it on to its highest levels. Our first aim is not to get liberal thinking done excellently, but to get it done at all. In a word, we must recognize that the drift of American life is against those forms of liberal teaching which seem to us most essential to its welfare.

The point just stated becomes more clear if we observe that the teaching process has two sides—the special, in which we as a people are abundantly successful, and the general which, with all our enthusiasm for it, we constantly misconstrue and defeat. We can train ordinary young people for special tasks and occupations in which they quickly "make good." And on this side, too, we can train leaders, can develop "experts" and "scholars" of the highest technical efficiency. But on the other side, that of liberal learning, our mind has not yet roused itself to activity. We do not feel the need, nor sense the beauty, of general understanding. And from this it follows that, in dealing with the deeper issues of life, its values, its beliefs, its fundamental institutions, we have neither intelligent living nor intelligent leading. It is here that the primary, urgent task of the liberal college lies. Our first question is, Can Americans, old and young, ordinary and extraordinary, be roused to undertake the task of understanding and evaluating American living? This does not mean that we are to ignore the other work, that of cultivating excellence, of training the best thinkers. It does mean that a democracy such as ours, by confusing the special and the general, has an infinite capacity for defeating its own deeper purposes. It means that the teachers of a democracy must be its critics, that in the training of its youth they must fight an unending battle against the blindly hostile forces of its popular drift. Their task is not so much to teach lessons whose value is recognized, as to create the recognition of value for insights which are essential to individual and social well-being. Under present conditions the primary aim of college teaching is a kind of spiritual remaking, a reshaping of fundamental attitude and interest.

If what has just been said is true, it follows not only that teaching is in large measure volitional, but also that it is very difficult. It does not admit of rough-and-ready, casual, or mechanical handling. It will not serve our purpose simply to offer fragmentary courses and then, if a student does not take them satisfactorily, to "flunk him out" of college. Under present social conditions, the general effect of such methods is to create in the student mind attitudes of unwilling and relatively dishonest conformity, devices for "getting by" the tests rather than for meeting them. In the face of this situation, the "preliminary hypothesis" of the advisers is that teaching should be personal, individual. We should bring to bear upon each student, according to his special needs, the influence of the individual teacher. And the statement here made applies to students whom we call "good" as well as to those who are "bad." Whatever the depths of their conventionality or the wildness of their variations from it, young Americans seem to us, at the present time, to need personal guidance in their attempt at the comprehension of good living. It is upon the basis of this belief that we have worked out our scheme of teaching arrangements.

The outline of the teaching plan can be briefly stated. First, the advisers, in accordance with their scheme of reference, present the course of study in the form of assigned readings to be done and papers to be written upon the reading. As a help to the student in his reading and his writing, three different kinds of meetings are arranged—(1) meetings attended by the class as a whole and by the advisers, (2) personal conferences of an adviser and a student, and (3) meetings of groups of about twelve students under the direction of an adviser. Each of these has a distinct and important part to play in the teaching process. The first and second have been developed into fairly satisfactory form.

The third is still very uncertain both in idea and in technique.

(1) Class meetings are held usually four or five times a week. Their number has tended to increase as the years have gone by. They are arranged, and usually conducted, by the adviser within whose special field the reading of the period falls. The primary intention of the meeting is that the adviser shall comment upon the reading, discussing it in such a way as to help the student in mastering it for himself. The peculiar nature of the purpose has sometimes been expressed in the statement that we wish the leader to give, not a "lecture," but a "talk." This means for us that he should always regard the reading as primary. He should not himself try to cover the same ground as the reading, giving his own systematic account of the material. He should not give to the students an organized interpretation of the reading, telling them, as it were, what the authors are saying and what their sayings mean. His function is rather to suggest points, to make comparisons, to raise questions, to talk with the students as if he and they were together reading the same books and were conversing about them. At practically all such meetings there is, of course, abundant opportunity for the asking of questions and for the informal discussion of difficult or disputed points. When, then, we say that the leader should not lecture, we mean that he should not take the primary responsibility for the interpretation of the reading, but should leave that to the individual student. It was said a moment ago that the technique of this meeting is now fairly well worked out. To say that is to say that advisers have in large measure overcome tendencies which were strong within them when the work began. Inevitably, at first, as we faced a group ranging from fifty to a hundred students and eight or ten of our colleagues, the impulse was strong within us to make a good presentation of the whole matter with which the reading had to do. Our tendency was to give the students the results of our own investigations and reflections rather than to help them in considering the subject matter presented by the books under discussion. The distinction here is a subtle one, but it is very real, and, with

much effort, the advisers have transformed their teaching methods in such a way as to keep for the student the sense of his primary responsibility for the making of his own education.

It should be noted at this point that we have had valuable help from outside lecturers who have come for a week or for shorter periods to present significant points of view. Usually these men have "lectured"; that is, they have given us additional material taken from their own books already written or in process of writing. And further, we have had most friendly and valuable help from members of the university faculty who have talked or lectured on matters within their special fields. Some of our best meetings have been conducted under their guidance.

(2) Individual conferences have been scheduled once a week for each student. Ordinarily they have been a half-hour in length, but in some cases this has been increased to three-quarters of an hour or an hour. Each full-time* adviser has, by lot, been assigned twelve or thirteen students whom he has kept for six weeks or more under his special direction. At the end of the period, new assignments have been again drawn, with arrangement for avoiding reassignment to the same adviser during the year.

The technique of the individual conference is at once more easy than that of the general class meeting, and more difficult. Here there is no strongly established habit, such as that of lecturing, to break down. There is, however, the task of selecting from an indefinite number of possibilities the essential things that can be done within a limited period. One must establish personal contact with the student, become acquainted with him; one must criticize the writing of the paper; one must discuss the investigation and interpretation which the paper expresses; one must lead the discussion on into the lines toward which it is implicitly directed; one must

---

*A full-time assignment at the Experimental College has been regarded as two-thirds of the regular university teaching assignment. A few of the advisers have been on half-time schedule with us, taking six advisees instead of twelve. In both cases the remaining time has been given to teaching "on the Hill" or to graduate study.

keep the different papers and their problems in mind in relation to the total enterprise in which the student is engaged; in a word, adviser and advisee must talk together as two students who have a common interest in a common undertaking. In such a relationship there are, on both sides, the emotional difficulties of shyness, reserve, hesitation, and the like. On the other hand, the contact is so immediate and so personal that is must be at every point genuine and direct. It has been very interesting to see how completely, in such meetings, evasions and concealments tend to disappear. There is no need of pretending on either side. There is no reason why the student should pretend to have done what he has not done, and there is no reason why the adviser should claim mastery over a field in which he too is only finding his way. It may safely be recorded that honesty and informality of personal relationship have been established to a remarkable degree.

And yet, admitting what has been said, it remains true that teaching by personal conference is a very difficult craft in which those who practice it should have long and careful training. One of its terrors, which is perhaps one of its greatest virtues, is that when time is being wasted, both teacher and pupil are painfully aware of the situation. The dangers which threaten it vary between two extremes. On the one hand, it may become for the student too subjective, may focus his attention too much upon himself, his attitudes, his difficulties, his possibilities. It is essential, as we have said, that the teacher should deal with the student in terms of his peculiarities of circumstance and nature. And when one does this there is always danger that the student will develop too much interest in these, will become interested in himself rather than in the world, the society, the objective situations and problems which it is his present business to study. And at the other extreme is the danger of being, in a bad sense, too objective and impersonal. The young man of eighteen or nineteen is, however he may have been externally smoothed down by the requirements of conformity, a curiously uneven and undeveloped person. And the temptation is strong upon a teacher who has standards of excellence to spend his time in defining and upholding those standards, in demanding conformity to the requirements of excellence without any regard to the present relation of his pupil to them. Between these two dangers, every conference wavers and vacillates. Each of them expresses, in extreme form, a legitimate and essential demand which the conference must meet, and, as between the two, no simple formula will in general terms express the proper balance. The situation varies with every student, with every change in his development, with every turn in the subject matter considered. If not an artist, the teacher is at least a craftsman, and he must learn by practice to adjust to each student his present material and his present purpose. So far as the personal conference is concerned, success in it, as we have already said, depends upon a peculiar combination of personal friendliness and impersonal criticism. We are teaching a student, but we are also teaching him in relation to demands made upon him by knowledge and beauty and high-mindedness, as objective factors in the human situation.

(3) The smaller group meeting has from the first been regarded as important, but it has thus far received much less careful attention than the other two parts of the teaching scheme. It is clear that much can be gained in attitude and habit of study if the students can be brought into active and intimate cooperation in dealing with it. The first arrangement for this purpose, still largely carried on in the freshman year, was that each adviser should hold a weekly meeting with his twelve advisees. There has been little general planning of these meetings, each adviser following his own inclinations or inventions as to procedure. And the results have shown the widest variations in success and failure. These have varied with the experience and the inclination of the adviser toward the leading of group discussion. And further, the outcome has been largely determined by chance as to whether or not the topics under consideration have found the kind of focus which brings different minds into active relationships as they deal with them. It has now,

however, become clear that the values of the small group meeting are too great to be neglected. In the year 1930-31, during the sophomore literature period, a promising beginning was made toward the shaping of a new program. The class was divided into small groups, each under the direction of an adviser. Each group assumed responsibility for presenting to the whole class some author or some phase of the literary study. Within the group, each member was by general vote assigned a special topic, and his results were passed upon by his fellows. The contributions of the groups were presented and discussed in general class meetings. Somewhat the same procedure is now being tried by a group which is carrying on a joint Regional Study of Madison. And further, the advisers are discussing plans for the extension of the arrangement. Group work of this character seems to us to give a valuable corrective to the subjective danger of the personal conference. But much more important, it contributes to the making of study an active social interest: It creates for the student social responsibility in the doing of his work. During the present year, the advisers hope to make definite progress in the attempt to give it a more important place in the teaching scheme.

In addition to this organized teaching program there have been many other meetings of a more or less informal sort. For example, on Monday morning of each week there has been held a meeting of the whole college which, in a secular way, has tried to accomplish the purpose of the college chapel of older days. Usually the chairman of the college has conducted the meeting, but at times other advisers have taken it in charge. The most frequent exercise has been that of reading from good literature, with comment on its form or content, but there have also been talks and discussions of questions of general interest and also consideration of immediate matters of faculty or student policy. There have been also a great number of informal personal conferences; meeting of small groups, sometimes in the form of clubs; and social gatherings in the homes of the advisers.

CHAPTER NINE

Gains and Losses

WE HAVE THUS FAR DEFINED a plan of teaching in terms of content and method. And now the primary question is, Does it work? Does it give education? The present chapter cannot attempt, in any complete form, a total evaluation. During these four years a very large part of the energy and attention of the advisers has gone not into teaching, but into the devising of a scheme of teaching. Our report is not that we have a scheme of teaching whose merits have been demonstrated, but that we have a plan which seems worthy of consideration by an American college of liberal arts.

I

First is the question of the time schedule of the student— the arrangements of his day and week. The fear is commonly expressed that the plan of the College involves too sudden a transformation from the controlled routine of the secondary school. Each week our student has four or five class meetings, a group meeting, a tutorial conference, as against the fifteen or sixteen classes usually scheduled for a college student. Further, there is no taking of attendance at class or group meetings. It can hardly be avoided at the individual conference. So the student has on his hand the task of arranging his own schedule. He himself must determine when he will study, when he will play, when he will get up and go to bed. He must work out for himself a plan of living, and take charge of its enforcement. Is not the burden too heavy, the change too swift?

Granted that the learning of self-direction is necessary, do you actually succeed in teaching it; do the students not take advantage of their freedom; do they not waste time and live in great disorder and confusion? This question deserves an answer which is honest, and so far as is possible, accurate. In the first place, most of the students, when they enter the college, have the lesson still to learn. And from this it follows that the mastering of it becomes one of the first and most urgent problems of their education. And for some of them it has proved necessary that they plunge themselves into the disorder and futility which come from the wasting of time so that they may discover for themselves how disappointing and unsatisfying shiftlessness is.

For the greater number, however, the problem does not take this form. Their task is rather that of well-disposed and sensible people who are given a new opportunity, a new kind of responsibility, and who thereupon proceed to build up the technique which it requires. But again, the question will be asked, does the giving of freedom pay; do the students, as time goes by, build up ability to manage themselves? And to this we can fairly answer that, as judged by fair standards of college achievement, the arrangement does justify itself.

If one asks how the lesson is taught, it must be remembered that, in addition to the response which freedom brings, there are two other sets of forces at work toward the accomplishing of the desired result: the personal contact with a teacher and the influence of the community. The second of these factors will be discussed in a later chapter. As to the first, the essential fact is that if a boy is shiftless, if he is negligent, if he has difficulty in organizing his time, he is, under our arrangement, in close touch with an older person who knows these facts, who talks with him about them, not as one who is trying to detect him in sin and to devise punishments to fit the crime, but as one who hates shiftlessness and such errors because they destroy essential human values.

To the question, then, Does this arrangement work? it seems fair to record the general answer that under the actual conditions of American academic life it works better than any other plan which is available. The lesson of self-direction is one which every self-respecting person must learn sooner or later. Our experience would seem to show that young Americans of eighteen to twenty are capable of learning it if given the chance. It will cost something, for a time, in other values; but it is worth more than it costs.

II

A second very serious question has to do with the advisers. Does not the plan of "personal" teaching make too heavy a demand upon them? Does not its expenditure of time and energy and interest interfere unduly with the other obligations of a teacher, his scholarly pursuits and his own cultivation of the power out of which teaching springs?

There can be no doubt that the drain upon the teaching staff has been heavy and at times exhausting. But a very large part of that burden has come not from teaching, but from having to devise the ways and instruments of teaching while the process is going on. The carrying on of an experiment entails burdens of work and of strain which do not belong to a developed teaching plan under normal conditions.

If such a system of teaching as we have outlined were normally and peacefully established, would it make heavier demands upon the teachers than does the usual American system, given the same ratio of students to teachers? A fair guess would be that the proposed system, normally running, would take less time in preparation and teaching; but that the time spent with the students would make heavier demands upon interest and energy. The personal scheme of teaching makes each instructor also, as it were, a dean, an adviser, taking cognizance of everything that enters into the development of his pupil; he is responsible not simply for presenting a subject, but for the education of the persons under his charge.

It seems fairly clear that the difference between the two teaching burdens is not decisive. Many of the advisers can record the fact that the creating of an experiment in the midst of a running university can be a killing experience. That, however, would still be quite consistent with the opinion that, with an integrated curriculum and tutorial teaching, greater teaching results can be gained at less teaching costs than in any other way.

III

The third point at which values conflict and, hence, serious question arises, is that of "non-expert" teaching. Each adviser in the college has, of course, his own special field of study. But as the college passes from phase to phase of Greek or American civilization, all the advisers share in the work, and, hence, each deals in turn with every line of study which is included in the curriculum. In other words, a teacher of art guides his successive groups of students in their studies of science, economics, politics, religion, literature, philosophy. An expert in science likewise leads the way, as well as he can, as his pupils fight for understanding of literature, philosophy, art, and all the rest. And it is at this point that the question at issue arises. Can a person teach effectively in a field of which he is not in some sense a master? Can a student be held to accuracy and comprehensiveness of treatment by a leader who has neither accurate nor comprehensive knowledge of the material with which both are dealing?

Now in this form the question must be answered, "No." There is a genuine loss in non-expert teaching. Other things being equal, the man who knows a field best should be best able to teach it. But in this case other things are not equal. There are many kinds of gain and loss to be measured. If we wish to see how these are balanced, it will be well to turn again for a moment, to the actual process of teaching.

Let us take a segment in which the college is dealing with some political phases of American life. Advisers who specialize in the field will have selected books. At four or five class meetings each week, during this period, the specialists will comment on the readings, will lead discussions, will help their students and fellow advisers to "place" and understand what they are reading. So far, of course, we have what would be called "expert" teaching. And now the "non-expert" process begins. In group meetings, in individual conferences, advisers and students talk together, considering the merits and shortcomings, the implications and significance, of the work which the student is doing.

It is evident that the specialist in art or in science who undertakes to help his pupils in their dealing with politics sees the field as an outsider. He sees it as any intelligent man, who has not devoted his life to its technical investigation, may be expected to see it. But if we are true to our definition of the function of the lower college, this is just the kind of understanding we wish our students to get. We are well aware that each student may have his eye on some special field into which some day he will go in pursuit of exact scholarship. But this is only one phase, one limited aspect of his liberal education. What of the other fields?

From the point of view which our argument is taking, it must be flatly said that the kind of understanding we are trying to teach in the lower college is that of the "outsider." Our primary task is to see, and to help students to see, subjects in their relations. We wish them to be intelligent about, to be able to read about, science and philosophy and politics and religion and art and literature and economics, rather than to develop a separate technical proficiency in each.

A group of advisers from different fields working together in intellectual comradeship, with each in turn taking the lead in the presentation of material, seems to us to have, for purposes of liberal teaching, a decided advantage over a group of specialists working separately and disconnectedly within their own fields. If we wish students to develop the kind of understanding which we call liberal, we must provide for it in the arrangement of our scheme of teaching. It is idle to ask students to see subjects in their relations if we ourselves deal with them separately and from within.

IV

There is still a fourth difficulty which is very closely related to the one just discussed. It is one which cannot fail to torment and terrify any adviser who has developed within his own field the habits and standards of scholarly technique.

Although the lower college uses scholarship, its methods and its results, for the developing of young Americans in intelligence, its primary task is *not* the education of scholars; it is the education of common men. And if we wish to estimate the results of college training, we must, primarily, measure it, not in terms of the kind of thinking which scholars do, but in terms of that thinking which all men are called upon to do in the ordinary relations of life. Can they use books for the guidance and enrichment of those relations? That is the essential question. It does not mean that books are to be used badly; it means only that they are to be used for an end which is not identical with scholarship.

For the sake of making clear this issue we may perhaps be allowed to use an illustration which in the modern world is now almost as trite as it is dreadful—that of the inventing of poison gases. In the contriving of these efficient devices for the destruction of human life, the chemist uses all the refinements of skill, of precision, of comprehensive information, of which his mind is capable. He does beautiful scholarly work. If, however, we ask, "Should such devices be used, should the nations engage in brutal, mutual self-destruction?" the chemist, as such, replies, "My studies give no answer to that question; it is not in my field." In whose field, then, does the question lie; shall it go by default? Now the plain fact is that no scholar, as such, not even the student of politics or of ethics, will take the responsibility for that decision. In the last resort we are driven back to the makers and enforcers of laws—in a democracy, to the legislators and the citizens of a community. And here we face exactly the dilemma which we are trying to illustrate.

The mental processes of the ordinary voter are not highly approved by men of scholarly training. The discussions of a legislature seem to them ill-informed, inaccurate, superficial, unscientific. The decisions of the "average voter" are intellectually quite disreputable. And so there arises the strain between the "expert" and the "common man." The latter must, in the making of practical decisions, have regard for all the results of scholarship. But he cannot possibly know them. He cannot know chemistry as the chemist knows it, and metaphysics as the metaphysician knows it; he cannot be a master of law and politics and economics and art and religion and all the rest. And especially he must be very inept in the face of the task of bringing together into some sort of intellectual order such fragments of these as he is able to gather and interpret. What a sorry mess his thinking is, when compared with the investigations of the scholars!

But why is it so bad? Is it because the mind of the common man is inferior in quality, his purpose less keen, than that of the scholar? The evidence available gives no support for that opinion. So far as one can see, the sufficient explanation is that "practical" questions are much more difficult than are those of the scholars. The latter group limits its field; it deals only with those matters for which its own technique is peculiarly suited; it cannot and will not deal with anything else. But in the world of human affairs, men cannot be so dainty in their choices; they must meet urgent problems as they come; they deal with problems, not because they can, but because they must.

For that reason, the results of the liberal training of freshmen and sophomores are to be measured or estimated chiefly, not in the field of accurate and limited scholarship, but in the field of inaccurate and uncertain human experience. As such they must always be, from the technical point of view, meager and disappointing.

Also, under present American conditions of school and social life, the results are far poorer in quality then they need be. Until our social order improves in this respect, every college, whether its methods be good or bad, must be content with a product which, under other social conditions, would condemn the work of the teacher as badly done.

Of course, as one stresses the values of common life as over against the claims of the technical scholar, one must be careful not to push the balance too far. After all, our chosen instrument in the college is scholarship; we teach by means of books. And further, every, or nearly every, student who engages in such study will discover within himself special powers, special forms of thinking, in which he can be peculiarly successful. In these cases it is the secondary purpose of the college to encourage the special interest and to develop it. But intelligence is not a by-product of scholarship. It is the end which scholarship serves.

CHAPTER TEN

Advisers and Students

ANYONE WHO IS CLOSELY in touch with the teaching process knows how difficult it is to give its inner quality by such external descriptions as the earlier chapters of this report have attempted. After all, the essential matter is that of the personal relation between the teacher and the pupil and of the mutual influences which pass between them. Such descriptions as have been given might take on life if the reader could spend some time in the midst of the process, so that the words might acquire color and immediacy and sharpness. Failing that, there are, however, records available for those who wish to understand and to appreciate the influences of the college and the responses of the students to them.

At the end of every assignment period, each adviser prepared an estimate of his pupils for the next advisers. At the end of each year these reports were summarized and then sent to the parents. There was much fumbling before these arrangements for "student estimates" were worked out, but they seem now to serve their purpose very well. It may be added that an essential feature of the letters to parents is a request that they will question or correct the estimates which the college has made and will, in turn, tell very frankly what they think has been the influence of the teaching upon their sons. Some of these replies have been exceedingly significant and helpful.

This chapter will now give four sets of advisers' reports as illustrative of the teaching problems which the advisers have faced and of the attitudes and methods adopted in dealing with them. The choice must be very arbitrary, and it should be clearly understood that it claims to represent nothing more than some different types of students with the corresponding different reactions of advisers to them. As one reads the reports, one should keep in mind that they are written as confidential notes among the advisers; they are often casual, even caustic, in manner, having been written within the freedom of a very closely knit and intimate community.

I
PETROFF

October

Petroff has worked as steadily and enthusiastically as anyone in my group. He is independent of mind without special keenness; in conference he is very much in earnest, eager to correct his mistakes and break open new paths. No worry that he will not do the required reading. His writing is quite bad—jumbled grammatically. I advise that he rewrite his papers or parts of them regularly for a time. Also he needs to be drawn out at group conference.

December

Has, I judge, no background of cultivation. Has his own world to make and with little sense of content or method. Probably not very able, but should develop a lot if suggestions are given him as he needs them and he is given the sense of getting on. One has to remember that most of his power toward study is as yet volitional rather than from understanding.

January

Petroff, once he is set firmly on a pathway and directions made clear, is enthusiastic, thorough, and (discounting a certain slowness of perception) competent. But once lost, he's just downright lost—and doesn't even go round in a circle.

76

He reads the material carefully, doggedly, and has a wide discussion experience—friends and advisers. His papers are lengthy, thorough—but he doesn't organize his material carefully enough and his writing is usually spotty and awkward. However, he cheerfully rewrote a 3,500 word paper and did a much better job.

March

His writing is rather awkward and his speech is full of colloquialisms. This, I presume, is due to home environment, though he tells me his father is a well-read man. His home is in a small agricultural town in the central part of the state. He should be encouraged to correct his speaking and writing. Possibly some mechanical exercises would help him.

There are no personal problems so far as I can tell. His mind is normally alert. He is sensitive to social problems and has few prejudices. He doesn't care for modern novels, though he likes literature. He reads more drama than any of the rest of my group.

June

A particularly thoughtful study of Aristophanes as a social critic and a full and well-organized "regional" study of Athens in 430 B.C. seemed to warrant a higher rating than earlier reports would suggest.

December

This boy is a very industrious and responsible student of Slavic immigrant parentage. His father is a skilled worker, and Joe has worked with him. I admire his industry and I think that he is developing good critical judgment. He reveals an increasing independent initiative in his work.

March

I have seen no more earnest student in the college, and few who read more widely.

His papers do not always live up to the promise of the work that goes into them. He usually glimpses the point—for example, the changes in American economic life reflected in

Wilson's program, or the one-industry limitations of his home town—but the glimpse is sometimes foggy. Somehow he lacks the ability to "put over" a clear, precise, unified paper that would deserve to be called excellent. In part his trouble is imagination and organization; he saw little or no continuity between the chapters of his Regional Study until I pointed it out to him. In part his difficulty is an inability to exclude irrelevant details. In part it is paucity of background brought from a small-town high school, and here I think the college has helped him and may continue to help him a great deal.

He writes better than most others, with only an occasional slip in idiom which he is pleased to have you point out.

(He was recommended for promotion to the junior class with a grade of B.)

II
JENSEN

October

Jensen's home is in Denver. He has had a wide prep school and military school experience since he was seven. He has never known a mother until recently when his father married again. The boy has plenty of assurance, has been about, is more or less a natural leader. He has been much rushed by the fraternities.

He did most of his reading, sometimes twice, but made little out of it. Part of the time—during fraternity rushing—he neglected his reading utterly, but continued to promise better. I think he will have to be checked up on closely, or he will wander away from the fold. I suspect that he will take the responsibility of being a loyal Wisconsinite, or something of the sort, too seriously.

Jensen's paper was sketchy, disorganized, brief. He certainly needs attention here.

In discussion he was active. He had the nerve to stand up to an opponent and, so to speak, face him down. But I must confess that his discussion was not noted for its penetration.

December

Jensen comes from a prosperous family. He relishes campus political activity. He is proud of his family, his city, his country—and his ability to "get things done." (Life is a series of neatly parceled, sharply defined duties to be met with promptness and self-discipline. Study is one phase of that life.)

This military-school attitude tells the story of his scholastic life here. He rolls up his sleeves, reads his "assignment," slams the book closed, and writes his paper. The papers are usually short, clearly thought out, but superficial. He wrote one very long paper which reflected a fine job of fact-finding and organization, but little critical thought. He swore he would never do a paper that thoroughly again—but he will if he is challenged—he will do anything on a "dare."

Lately his blithe acceptance of the social order has been undergoing changes; he begins to doubt the divinity of our political mechanism—though the industrial system is beyond reproach.

January

Jensen did some fairly good work in the *Republic*. He was a bit hard for me to reach in a vital way. My impression of him is that he has average abilities and pretty broad interests. He is apparently very interested and is liking it very much here. If we can get him to dig into some of the material, he might develop surprisingly well.

May

Jensen admits that he was a narrow-minded young business man until he came here and met the communists, et al. He is fond of one student with whom he argues for hours about social injustice and the remedies. At the same time, his life centers a great deal in his fraternity, where I judge the intellectual light shines a little dimly.

He has been irregular in conferences and with his papers. He is confused in his thinking, with little aptitude for abstract questions. Sleeps late. A sleek horse that needs a constant gadfly.

June

Classification: C–

General summary: Jensen this year attempted such a varied and active extracurricular program that his life in the college was casual, concerned only with the mechanical grinding out of his assignments. He is capable of far better work than he accomplished. His attendance at college and class meetings was wretched. His outstanding qualities are vigor, pride, and a high sense of duty.

Quality of work: He was rigidly loyal in doing mechanically the assigned reading and papers, though he read almost solely in order to write. His papers were neat, moderately well-written, and superficial. His final conference-exam indicated that he has grasped the high spots of the Greek study—and that he has a mind superior to the use of it he has made this year.

Remark: He should return next year determined to attend all meetings, give up most of his activity work, and give his intelligence a chance.

October

Came fairly regularly to the lab for ten days, but did very little work. His tendency was to play around. Was barred from laboratory for the last two weeks. Should have been able to do good work. Needs prodding or should be let out.

December

What can be done about his work here is a question. He is courteous and, I believe, frank. I guess he has moments of good intentions about study. At all times he wants to be well thought of and successful. But I doubt if he can ever know what it is all about. He couldn't get at what Henry Adams way saying, so he wrote nothing. Knowing he had an interest in horses, I proposed that he write a paper on the evolution of the horse for his science period. He did. He made a sort of outline sketch from a technical book on the subject, cataloguing periods and species with labels which, I fear, he understood no better than I. On the whole, I think he is wasting his time.

April

Jensen stayed in the poetry group, in spite of his distaste for poetry of whatever sort, because he thought he ought to get acquainted with it and try to get something out of it. He read a good deal of Robinson and achieved some measure of understanding of him. His paper was unambitious and fair in quality. I like this fellow; he has a long way to go—just fair abilities.

(He was recommended for promotion to the junior class but on probation.)

III
BUEHLER

October

First conference: Absent. Learned later that he was in the infirmary for a week with an injured leg.

First paper: Not handed in. He did the reading, so we decided to let this paper go.

Second conference: Have failed to come to grips with this chap yet. He has done some reading, but his interest is not particularly stimulated. I have not had enough contact to make estimate of his powers. He seems pleasant, willing, and interested a little.

Third conference: A very quiet and reserved person, difficult for me to draw out. He seems to be working well. Presented an ambitious outline for paper on foreign relations.

Fourth conference: Absent. Largely my fault. Rather an elusive chap. Failed to make any vital contact with him. He is shy and reserved.

November

Buehler was one of my best advisees: earnest, quiet, self-possessed, inquisitive. His comments are always honest and independent, with sometimes canny insight. His papers have been clear, sane, complete. He is interested in probing below the surface to study motives and causes. He writes well and should be encouraged to keep a record of his intellectual response to his reading. It isn't easy to get to know him; he is reserved and doesn't wear his ability on his sleeve.

January

This boy has a serious and, I think, rather brooding mind, but I imagine he is prone to daydreaming rather than accomplishment. Through most of the group discussions he sat looking out the window without taking any active part. However, in the last meeting he seemed to have many things to say, but was somewhat retiring about taking the floor. He seems to have a realistic mind that is impatient with anything suggesting absolutes and that is quite penetrating in argument. In short, he has considerable intellectual capacity. What he needs is to be constantly encouraged and led on. He did nothing of moment; but, apparently feeling impelled to do something for me, he wrote off a paper on caste systems that contained some good suggestions, but which did not follow them up and which was in general hardly a serious piece of work. He missed one conference, but was very careful about arranging to make it up.

March

Reads widely, and often carelessly. Capable of care and sometimes uses it. Writes reasonably well; somewhat explosive. Good participation in discussion.

Needs to study more and read less. A good "spirit" and a good mind, in need of some "discipline."

May

Fred Buehler has talent. His year has not been one of the careful scholarship of which he is capable. He has been groping, introspecting, rationalizing. He is now a vigorous, active futilitarian.

(Probably with his appetite for knowing and his intuition, he was painfully startled, when thrown with the Experimental College group, to discover how highly self-over-evaluated he was when he came here.)

He was regular at all meetings, read the science and philosophy material. He wants to work on more subtle and difficult problems than the group, but he never really makes a complete, specific, scholarly accomplishment.

He handed in no paper.

June

Classification: B+

General summary: Buehler this year has been very young, very intelligent, very introspective—therefore very confused. The consequence has been a certain aloofness. The topics suggested for the whole class have usually seemed too simple for grand conceptions—so he has often stormed off on expeditions of his own—and usually arrived nowhere. Perhaps some would call this rebellion. He has spent a profitable year—providing he moves along a natural adolescent development and turns to disciplined scholarship next year.

Quality of work: When he completes a paper, it is a splendid one. His final paper was the product of careful scholarship and a noteworthy accomplishment for a college freshman.

Remarks: He has probably hovered this year at times on the dangerous mood. But I do not consider him a problem.

November

Laboratory attendance good. A good student, well fitted for this kind of work.

December

Buehler is a most unusual student. He has grown up among the Amish communities near Akron; and I suspect in a household of fairly circumscribed outlook in religion and other matters. I also surmise that he has packed an immense amount of study and reading into the last two years without developing the air of sophistication and arrogance which some other boys acquire. He is somewhat shy and questions his own ability; he really needs more encouragement and self-confidence. I think there are the makings of a quite unusual type of research scholar in him. The chief difficulty is the possibility of his not seeing any tangible interest or activity to which he should direct his energy during the next two or three years; he is likely to fall under too strong a sense of disillusionment in his studies of philosophy and the borders of science, and the adviser should try to keep him concerned with "human" interests and activities.

February

Work this period: His work in the prescribed material is seldom so important as the work he carries on independently, I believe. He is not greatly interested in economic problems of a general nature, though he has a good grasp of the economic situation of his own Amish group in Ohio. His paper on the economic depression was unfinished, though as it stood it it was fuller and better than any other paper I received. He complains that he can never finish a paper because his reading and thinking succeed in making the immensity and the hopelessness of solving each problem evident to him. He is inclined to want to go into business later, because academic work makes one dissatisfied with everything. And yet he is happier this year than last. I think he is best left to follow his own course, with whatever suggestions an adviser can find to help him in the work he is pursuing. He says that he has won his way through the glib phase of sophisticated shallowness. And I believe he is right.

Reading: He reads about two non-prescribed books a week. He has read a good bit on sex.

Social adjustment: He has a few good friends and very few acquaintances. I think it would be well if he did make more social contacts. He should be having a few dates.

March

Regional Study: B+

Buehler delved quite deeply into the geology, geography, and the soils of his region, linking these with early settlement and more recent developments. He showed both perseverance and originality in digging up this background material and in using it to interpret the life of that section. His paper is well written and reveals quite a grasp of the situation, rather belying his modesty. Unfortunately, Buehler was unable to complete certain parts of his paper. Having taken time to do thorough work on earlier portions, he tells less than he could about the Amish, etc.

June

A very able boy who is very pleasant to deal with. He is unusually reflective and dreamy. He has been reading a great deal on the modern sciences. In conversations he is likely to be rather incoherent or perhaps fragmentary. He impresses one as understanding much more than he can communicate. His Adams paper was in a rudimentary stage. (An unfortunate illness has prevented him from doing his best this year.) But as it was, it showed thought and penetration. I am sorry he could not complete the work, for I should be anxious to see a finished job of his.

(Buehler was recommended for promotion to the junior class with a grade of B+.)

IV
SCHULZ

November

Not always up-to-date on reading, due mostly to work outside (to earn way through school). Writing all right. Takes part in group discussions—interested, intelligent. Probably hasn't the best of backgrounds. His interests are general; eager for knowledge; likes the college. His social adjustment seems all right; is handicapped in this line by having to work. Likable. He has no outside university activities but is taking a course "on the Hill"—French. Papers are well done.

February

Schulz was easily one of the best men in my group. Alert, active and conscientious, persistent and thoughtful. He has a fair background of reading and has worked steadily to enlarge it during this period. His work in art was excellent; he enjoyed sketching and did some interesting work; also tried his hand at clay modeling. His biography of Euripides was a thoughtful piece of work.

His notebook on literature was especially good, with well-thought-out comments on wide reading. Not too keenly critical, but analytical in a good, sound way. He is especially interested in drama.

Whatever is done for him will be appreciated and made good use of.

June

A serious-minded, hard-working student, rather puzzled as to what he wants to do. He tried working in a business house for a time before entering the university, but did not like it. He wants intensely to be "educated." There is no doubt that he is able, though his writing is slightly stilted and does not, I think, wholly do him justice. At present he is thinking of becoming a psychiatrist and has talked to Dr. Lorenz on the subject. He has the problem of supporting himself.

November

Schulz is tackling Wheeling for his Regional Study. He read *Middletown* early, last summer, and gathered a good deal of material on Wheeling before returning to Madison this fall. His interest is primarily in the industrial aspects of his region.

Though he worked hard at it, Schulz had quite serious trouble with the mathematics involved in the early weeks of the science period. But he kept at it and came through the first weeks pretty well. As the science period continued, he became increasingly interested, both in a generous number of laboratory experiments and in his reading on science. His final paper was a good, thoughtful piece of work—on scientific method in atomic research.

Does more than the minimum, though he works in the refectory several hours a day. One of the best students in my first group.

January

Good man—hard, cheerful worker. Attitude very satisfactory; despite handicap of money shortage, etc., immense courage and resiliency. Very rapid development. Weak in accuracy, presentation, and taste, but promising material. He deserves every encouragement.

April

A really critical and appraising mind, mature, fair-minded. He should go far, but a very serious financial handicap plus a deep feeling of responsibility for helping his parents may prevent further formal college work. His Regional is an excellent study of Wheeling; and his study of the Chinese Eastern Railroad is a gem, as is his literary notebook. He is a great credit to the college.

June

Schulz has gained more from the college than almost any student I have seen. In my opinion, he has acquired sufficient intellectual stimulus and technique to last him a lifetime. He has read widely during these two years and clearly intends to read much more, even though he must leave college for the business world.

He has learned to look at economic and political abuses from a detached and relatively scholarly point of view, and seems clear in his mind as to what values he wants to get in life.

He has been unusually hard-working and intelligent. His steadiness is attractive as combined with his willingness and ability to criticize.

Lack of money is his reason for not going on in college.

(Schulz was recommended for promotion to the junior class with a grade of A.)

These four sets of records illustrate four different groups of students which it may be worthwhile to characterize in a few words.

The first type is that of the small-town or village or

country boy, evidently of good stock, often of second-generation American residence. He is, at the beginning, undeveloped in cultural ways, knows little of the world of men or of letters, has trouble in speech or writing or both, is impressed, and sometimes depressed, by the greater facility and cleverness of more sophisticated companions. He may have had a fairly good record in high school, but he is still the typical, small-town, Middle Western youth. But he is responsive; he knows with more or less clearness that there is another world into which study will take him, and he is willing to work his way toward it. If he is very wise, he knows that he need not give up his old world when entering the new. This is, on the whole, our most satisfactory student and the one to whom the methods of the college seem best fitted. It has been one of the tragedies of the college that the hostility of a surrounding community has kept from us young men of this type. We have had many of them, quite enough for experimental purposes, but not enough to realize our hope that we might have a student body which would be representative of the colleges and universities of the Middle West.

The second group is that of the socially successful student. He is able to make his way in terms of clothes and manners and is interested in doing so. He belongs to what one commonly calls the "fraternity type." He is successful in external ways and is interested in the men who get on in the world. He is very hard to deal with because "success" has already taken on a meaning for him, and the advisers find established in him a social influence against which they very often struggle in vain. Such young men are usually courteous to their teachers, but they do not take them seriously. In this connection it may be said that between a residential college and a fraternity there is inevitably a serious and harmful rivalry. Each is, in social ways, trying to capture the imagination and will of the student, to lead him into certain ways of living. And in general, if the fraternity succeeds the college fails. Apart from a number of striking exceptions, it is worthy of note that among the students who have failed to respond actively to the teaching influence of the college an unduly large proportion is found among the members of fraternities.

Still a third group is that of the able, relatively well-trained and serious students who, nevertheless, are inclined to have their freedom during the college years, to go their own way, to engage in "activities," to read according to their own interests and preoccupations rather than according to the fixed schedule which the advisers may prescribe. Such young men vary much in ability and also in reasonableness of attitude—perhaps in clearness of perception of the kind of rebellion they are carrying on. They always, of course, trouble the minds of their advisers who have laid down work for them to do, and there is a constant temptation to try to whip them into shape. In dealing with these students, obviously the chief task of the adviser is to get them to see, as clearly as possible, the meaning of what they are doing. Undoubtedly they waste much time. But undoubtedly, also, such experiences are often necessary for youth which is shaking itself free from controls and restraints. Perhaps they do not waste as much time as do those who try to prevent them from living their own lives.

The fourth group is that of the able and well-prepared students who, in one way or another, have become ready for eager cooperation with teachers and the teaching system. This does not mean that they accept instruction with docility, but that they are untroubled in mind about teaching and so are ready to cooperate with the men who are teaching them. These are, in every respect, the good students. They appeal to teachers because many of them are already in process of becoming, in their turn, teachers. They are scholarly in interest and physiologically, emotionally, socially, intellectually adjusted to scholarly living. They are less tantalizing than the third group and more gratifying in technical ways than the first group. Between them and their teachers there quickly develops a friendly comradeship.

It was said a moment ago that, among these four groups, it is the first for which the methods of the Experimental

College seem best adapted. And in a sense this is true. Nothing is more gratifying than to see the apparently ill-trained, unpromising fellow find his way, take new courage, lose the sense of being awkward and inferior to his fellows. But in a deeper sense, the method of the college is dominated by the demand that all four of these types shall be equally regarded and cared for. The most important feature of the "personal conference" method is its flexibility, its readiness to deal with each student according to the needs of his own immediate situation. And in a democratic scheme of education, this flexibility is essential. It is sometimes said that democratic education is necessarily mass education, that the demand for equal opportunity for all inevitably leads to uniformity and mechanization of teaching procedure. But nothing could be further from the truth. For the teacher, the essential principle of democracy is that of the worth and significance of the individual pupil. And from this it follows that not only each group, but each separate member of each group, shall have his own separate and distinct teaching. The young man who has been driven by family success and by social superficialities into an external and superficial view of life must be dealt with accordingly. He needs "inner" teaching, and the welfare of society demands that he be given it. To dismiss him from college as unfit is to abandon an essential task. We must learn how to teach him. So too, the young fellow who is resisting us because he has, or wants to have, purposes of his own must, in the proper sense, be taught. However far he may wander afield, however foolish he may be in action and in idea, he must be made to realize that fundamentally we accept his decisions, that we approve what he is doing. And the "good" student must also be taught. We must keep him from becoming dependent, must make him critical even of the scholarship which we use and of the ends for which we use it. In a word, we must take students as we find them, and must give to each such friendship and such assistance as personal acquaintance enables us to devise.

There is one other group of students, the mention of

which will throw light upon the teaching problem and teaching methods. Its members are found in all the four groups given above, and some of them cannot be placed in any one of these. They are the young men who, for one reason or another, are under physiological and emotional strains which interfere seriously with healthy living and successful learning. The state may vary from minor forms of laziness, moodiness, and depression down to definite and serious abnormalities of attitude and behavior. What shall be done with these students? It is now recognized that under the present conditions of American life these disturbances are to be expected at all ages and in all periods of growth. And probably the time of late adolescence is especially fruitful in them. It would seem than that any teaching scheme must be ready and equipped to deal with students classifiable in this group. In the very nature of the case, the Experimental College has had more than the usual share of disturbed and more or less abnormal students. "Problem" sons have been sent to the college, and also they have wished to come because of its apparent readiness to give them the special consideration which they needed. And as a result of this, a great deal of the energy and time of the advisers has been given to the attempt to help these students who are so especially in need of help. No layman who undertakes a psychiatric task can be very confident of his ability to do it well, but it can safely be said that the expenditure of time and energy involved seems to the advisers fully justified both by necessity and by results.

CHAPTER ELEVEN

The Health of the Community

IN A FAMOUS PASSAGE in his *Idea of a University*, John Henry Newman gives his judgment of the relative importance, in a teaching scheme, of the "determining conditions" of study.

> I protest to you, Gentlemen, that if I had to choose between a so-called university which dispensed with residence and tutorial superintendence, and gave its degrees to any person who passed an examination in a wide range of subjects, and a university which had no professors or examinations at all, but merely brought a number of young men together for three or four years, and then sent them away, as the University of Oxford is said to have done some sixty years since, if I were asked which of these two methods was the better discipline of the intellect—mind, I do not say which is *morally* the better, for it is plain that compulsory study must be a good and idleness an intolerable mischief—but if I must determine which of the two courses was the more successful in training, moulding, enlarging the mind, which sent out men the more fitted for their secular duties, which produced better public men, men of the world, men whose names would descend to posterity, I have no hesitation in giving the preference to that university which did nothing, over that which exacted of its members an acquaintance with every science under the sun. . . . How is this to be explained? I suppose as follows: When a multitude of young men, keen, open-hearted, sympathetic, and observant, as young men are, come together and freely mix with one another, even if there be no one to teach them, the conversation of all is a series of lectures to each, and they gain for themselves new

ideas and views, fresh matter of thought, and distinct
principles for judging and acting, day by day. . . . Let it be
clearly understood, I repeat it, that I am not taking into
account moral or religious considerations: I am but saying
that that youthful community will constitute a whole, it will
embody a specific idea, it will represent a doctrine, it will
administer a code of conduct, and it will furnish principles of
thought and action. It will give birth to a living teaching,
which in the course of time will take the shape of a self-
perpetuating tradition, or a genius loci, as it is sometimes
called, which haunts the home where it has been born, and
which imbues and forms, more or less, and one by one, every
individual who is successively brought under its shadow.*

Now if Newman is right—as one can hardly doubt that he
is—then this report has reserved to the last a phase of the
educational problem which is at least as important as those
already considered. It has dealt with the course of study and
the methods of teaching. We must now take up what has
happened in the attempt to form such a community, to
establish such a set of social influences as Newman finds so
important in its effect upon the intellectual development of a
group of students. What then shall we say of the determining
conditions of freshman and sophomore study as illustrated
by the experience of the Experimental College?

The preliminary hypothesis of the advisers at this point
was that conditions of residence and association should be so
arranged that intellectual and social relations would fuse
together—that advisers and students would become a closely
knit intellectual community. It was hoped that the cleavage
between "studies" and "activities," so common in undergraduate life, might be broken down so that books and their
meanings might be given drive and zest by the liveliness of
undergraduate loyalty, while, on the other hand, the
"activities" would be deepened and refined and enlightened
by active forces of appreciation and intelligence. The intention was that young men should learn to play as if they were

---

*Cardinal John Henry Newman, *The Idea of a University*, new ed. (New York:
Longmans, Green and Co., Inc., 1947), pp. 128-30.

intelligent and responsible human beings and should learn to work as if they were free and joyous comrades in a thrilling enterprise.

To this end it was arranged that all the students should live in the same dormitory, rooming side by side and eating in the same refectory. And further, the advisers were given offices or studies in the same building. At first only a part of the dormitory was reserved for the college, but it was hoped that in the second year the whole building might be taken over so that the community might feel that it had a home of its own.

The record of the experience of the college in this field is, on the external side, one of constant and rather bitter disappointment. The hope of taking over the whole building was not realized. The group has not, therefore, been separated off as a complete residential unit. And the building itself, planned before the college had been thought of, has proved sadly unsuited to the making of an intellectual community. Apart from a very restricted use of one of the dining rooms in the refectory, there has been no common place in which the college could assemble in social ways. Even for purposes of class and college meetings we have had no room of our own, but only a classroom, or at times two of these loaned with great kindness by the College of Agriculture, but nevertheless as little suited to the intention of the college as rooms could possibly be. One may fairly say that, so far as building arrangements are concerned, the preliminary hypothesis has hardly been tested at all.

And the situation with regard to the surrounding community has been equally unfortunate. From the beginning the college was involved in strains and conflicts which were destructive of its own healthy and normal social development. During the first two years its presence on the campus was keenly resented by many students, by members of the faculty, and by administrative officers. And from this feeling there developed much misguided and destructive controversy. The "freedom" inherent in the teaching method of the college was seen in vivid contrast to various requirements imposed upon other students and was sharply criticized. The college was felt to be critical of the university which had established it, to be hostile to the loyalties and traditions of the university community; and this supposed hostility was repaid in kind.

Beginning with the second year, there were constant rumors that the experiment would soon be abandoned; the number of students from Wisconsin dropped in two years from forty-five to eleven. More and more the group became outsiders and aliens, and the college itself an invasion to be tolerated only so long as might be necessary. In a word, the external situation was such as to make practically impossible the task of establishing a happy and well-poised group life. These statements are not made in a spirit of faultfinding against the surrounding community. In any such difficult situation mistakes are made on both sides, and it would be idle to attempt here to determine their distribution.

But there have been also serious difficulties within the group itself, increased by outside pressures, but yet existent and active quite apart from those pressures. It was quickly, and not surprisingly, evident that the students who came to the college were markedly individualistic, that they would strongly resist influences working toward group solidarity. And again certain cleavages quickly appeared, cutting across the student body and dividing it into parts which were uninterested in each other and, at times, definitely uncongenial. It may be worthwhile to explain each of these difficulties briefly. The "cleavage" situation will be considered first.

Along three lines, the college body quickly suffered separation. First, there was the break between fraternity and non-fraternity men. The fraternity men went actively into the life of small social groups in the outer university; they found there loyalties of an intimate and compelling sort; in many cases, the fraternity house became their home rather than the college dormitory. But to other students, to join a fraternity seemed to mean a departing from the college or at least a serious dividing of one's loyalty. These men, being invited to join a fraternity, refused the invitation or, not being asked, recognized the fact that they were different from their fellows who had established such connections. A second cleavage was that between "radicals" and "conservatives." In the college group, the greater portion were, as in any assemblage of young Americans, of the conservative type. But the minority of radicals was undoubtedly larger than is usual in such groups. Many of the students came from homes and social surroundings where poverty or free discussion or both had aroused active rebellion against existing institutions. For a time the college had a very active group of communists in its midst. Between these radicals and their fellows there were the customary difficulties of understanding, accentuated perhaps by the constancy and closeness of their association. Still a third division was racial, that between Jews and Gentiles. The percentage of Jews was, quite naturally, unusually large, and it has tended to increase. And further, Jews and their Gentile confreres came to the college life with all the customary prejudices, fears, hostilities which this cleavage brings. It was not to be expected that they would easily fuse together into membership in a common college family.

Though slight at first, the separation between fraternity and non-fraternity men has widened rather than narrowed with the passing of time. Fewer students with fraternity inclinations have entered the college, and the disposition not to join has apparently also strengthened. The proportion of fraternity membership has diminished until now, at the beginning of the year 1931-32, only eight students out of sixty-six are fraternity members. In the two other cases, however, there has been definite and gratifying success in breaking down separation and establishing acquaintance.

Radicals and conservatives have come to see one another more clearly, and they talk and study and play together untroubled by imagined barriers. One can even see students shifting from one side of the line to the other, and then back again, and accepting the transitions as natural experiences for persons engaged in the business of liberal education. And this being true, the words *radical* and *conservative* have lost their sting; they express important differences of ideas, but they no longer smack of personal and social antagonism.

And in like manner, the relations of Jews and Gentiles have slowly but very steadily and very greatly improved. In fact, it is amazing to see how completely the distinction is lost from sight. When people know one another in common terms, the difference between Jew and Gentile becomes no different from that between English and Scotch, Italian and German. It is enlightening for Gentile young men to discover, not by being told but by actual contact, that Jews are like other people. They are bright or dull, industrious or lazy, gay or sober, generous or selfish, just as their fellows are. The only difference they seem to have from others is that they are thought to be different and that they suffer the consequences of being so interpreted. We have spoken of this as a gratifying result. And surely, from the point of view of education, the statement is justified. Nothing can be more typical of education gone astray than a teaching which instructs pupils with regard to the races of men, which studies human nature scientifically and yet leaves both teachers and pupils filled with the prejudices and the meannesses of racial antipathies. When ideas and attitudes can be joined together in so external a way as that, one need have no hesitation in declaring the ideas dead, the education ineffectual.

The interference of "individualism" with the unification of the college community has taken many amusing as well as serious forms. It made its first appearance a few weeks after the college opened. The students were invited to form an organization of their own to take charge of their common interests and to deal with the advisers and any other groups with whom they might have relations. For a month or more they debated plans of organization with great inventiveness in devising schemes of action and in suggesting improvements of those already invented. And in the end they decided not to organize at all. They seemed to prefer not to recognize any common business or, if it should be forced upon them, to deal with it only as each specific occasion might call forth its appropriate response. Finally a council was established and it is now fairly active in directing the social life of the college. But its chief activity has been that of bringing in outside lecturers and arranging meetings with them. In times of emergency, however, when library books were missing or when money was needed for special purposes, it has shown itself capable of vigorous action.

We have spoken so far of the external side of the college community—of its organization and activities. Here, as we have said, the story is one of difficult and slight achievement. On the inner side, however, a different picture can be drawn. Newman, in the passage previously quoted, speaks of "a living teaching, which in the course of time will take the shape of a self-perpetuating tradition, or a genius loci, as it is sometimes called, which haunts the home where it has been born, and which imbues and forms, more or less, and one by one, every individual who is brought under its shadow." Now in this sense there can be no doubt that the Experimental College has had a decided effect upon its pupils. They are very keenly aware of being members of the college; they think of themselves in terms of it. Their education is for them something distinctive which marks them off as a group from others who are having a different education. And the important point is that the difference which arouses their interest is an intellectual one. They think of the community to which they belong, not in the ordinary social terms of this or that "activity," but in terms of a kind of studying, a content of understanding, an intellectual method of approach. And so far as this is true, it means that the attempt to fuse together the intellectual and the social has succeeded. The college has become, in the minds of its students, an intellectual community. This does not mean that all the students devote themselves with full vigor to their studies. It does mean that they measure themselves and their fellows, their successes and their failures, in terms of the values toward which studies are directed.

And with this statement made, it may now be permissible to touch with brighter colors the picture which was so darkly painted in the early part of the chapter. One of the best ways to do this would be to refer the reader to the yearbook which was published by the first class at the end of the college's first year. One will get there the sense of a community which has been actively engaged in the giving of Greek and American plays, in the arranging of lectures and discussions, in the carrying on of discussion and study clubs in law, science, art, philosophy, medicine, politics, in the management of a workshop in painting, modeling, and other forms of expression in writing and criticism. These activities have not been carried on regularly. They have risen up and died down. But two things can fairly be said about them. At many points they have achieved quite remarkable quality. For example, the Greek plays were as student performances surprisingly successful. And further, taken all together, they have expressed in social forms a very lively and creative interest in the values of intelligence and appreciation. With proper facilities, indefinitely more could have been done. But even as conditions have been, one may say that, within itself, in relation to its own values, the college has become a genuine community.

A question with regard to determining conditions has often been raised among the advisers. "If we were starting again, under conditions as we now know them, would we again insist upon the requirement of dormitory residence; is the preliminary hypothesis sustained at this point?" And the discussion of the advisers would seem to indicate that, if another beginning were made in the same external situation, they would prefer to give up the dormitory arrangement. Especially would this be true if they were able to substitute for it central meeting rooms adequate for their purpose, with offices and studies and library so related as to serve as proper headquarters for an intellectual community. But if this decision were made, it is certain that it would be made reluctantly. It could be made only on the ground that present dormitory accommodations, not being planned for the purposes of the college, are quite unsuited to it. If, however, it were possible to build a dormitory with the scheme of instruction in mind, if these two sets of educational arrangements could be planned and executed from a common point of view, there can be no doubt as to what the preference of the advisers would be.

One of the most urgent needs of the American college—one might almost say a desperately urgent need—is that of fusing together the intellectual and social activities of the students. And to this end no method seems more promising than that of bringing together into a residential unit teachers and students who are engaged in the same intellectual enterprise. It is essential that American students know each other intellectually and that they know their teachers personally. No external educational influence is so powerful in the molding of a young man as membership in a group which, commanding his interest and his admiration, becomes for him a way of living. And to this end, it will not do, as is so commonly arranged in the dormitory schemes which are now being established, to bring together students from different fields and different departments. In the activities of liberal education, the different tastes, capacities, trainings, backgrounds, and expectations give quite enough of variety. What is needed is that the community find its life centering about a common course of study, a common set of problems, a common human situation. The effect of this is to give to the casual conversation, the easy association of students, an educational value which is wholly lost if one's dormitory friends or fraternity house mates are studying in different fields. If one member of a group is studying physics and another art and another economics, then it follows almost inevitably that neither physics nor art nor economics will be easily talked about. The group must search for matters of common interest outside the field of studies altogether. The studies become private and socially uninteresting pieces of work. But if the whole group is engaged in the same attempt at learning then every aspect of the social living becomes steeped in the common purpose. Men breathe it in, eat it in, play it in, smoke it in, study it in, laugh it in, discuss it in until education becomes what it ought to be—not a set of imposed, demanded, external tasks, but a form of human living and association, the natural and inevitable growth of a healthy organism in a congenial environment. Not one of our liberal colleges seems yet to have explored the possibilities of this kind of educational influence.

IV.

Suggestions

CHAPTER TWELVE

Counterproposals

AS THE ADVISERS have worked at the problem of constructing and organizing the Athens-America curriculum, there have been suggested many variations from it of a more or less radical sort. Some of these are in the form of carefully prepared memoranda. Others are less explicitly formulated but have often reappeared as possible ways of overcoming or avoiding difficulties inherent in the "preliminary hypothesis." This report can give little more than a listing of these suggestions. They are presented, it should be understood, merely as undeveloped notions. They fall into three groups.

1. There are two suggestions, often mentioned in the first years of the college, which have now practically disappeared from our discussion. The first of these was that the order of the two civilizations studied should be reversed, that America should be taken up in the first year and that Athens in the second. The suggestion was grounded in the fear that the life of Greece would seem to a freshman dead and strange and unmeaning. But the suggestion has lost force as the meaning of the words *studying Athens* has been transformed. It rested on the supposition that our purpose in the first year was to "learn" an ancient civilization. One might well reject it if that supposition were true. But as explained previously, our plan has been far from that. The study of Athens has become a first step in the attempt to understand contemporary America. In that form there seems to most of us no lack of vividness or vitality of interest.

The second passing suggestion was that the curriculum

should be organized about a number of "Great Books" rather than about two civilizations. In the midst of the confusion and blocking of the second year, when the advisers were unable to select and to relate books of first-rate quality bearing upon America, this suggestion had for them a strong appeal. "Let a student read," they said, "Shakespeare, Kant, Marx, Newton, Spinoza, Darwin; let him see their thoughts in their own words; he will then discover modern intelligence at work in the minds of the men who have created it." But, for two reasons, the plan lost its interest. First, it seems practically impossible to make an organized scheme of teaching out of the writings of unrelated "great men." And, second, the difficulties out of which the suggestion grew have largely disappeared. The Athens-America course has taken working form. The preliminary hypothesis has, at least, become a practical curriculum. The tension of perplexity has therefore been slackened.

2. The suggestions in the second group accept the two-civilization plan of study. Their attack is, however, focused upon the selection of Athens as the subject for the first year. Each of them proposes for this the substitution of another episode in human civilization. Europe in the medieval times and Europe in the Renaissance have both been suggested, with the understanding that in each case either the total situation or some community or episode within it might be studied. Other proposals are Europe in the Industrial Revolution, Europe in the eighteenth century, and England in the nineteenth century. There can be no doubt that in the hands of a group of teachers who see it in its significance for contemporary human living, any one of these "situations" might be used to give the first step in the lower college program. In each case the teaching problem will be found to be that of combining two factors: (1) the literature of the period and (2) the making of a scheme of reference for the interpreting of human living. It is not enough that the period or the civilization be significant. That significance must be well stated for the student in the writings of the situation itself. In the cases of eighteenth-century Europe and

nineteenth-century England, very promising beginnings have been made toward the organizing of the literature for that purpose. Whether or not any one of these suggestions would prove preferable to the Athens plan could be determined only by actual experimentation. It seems to us exceedingly important that some of these experiments be worked out and tried.

3. A very interesting variation from the Athens-America plan was the suggestion that the study of contemporary America should run throughout the two years, but, that in each phase of the study, reference should be made to some other European or American episode which seemed of peculiar significance. Thus, while studying modern art, one might turn back to Athens or to the Italy of the Renaissance; when discussing industry one would go back to the Industrial Revolution; when exploring American politics, one would turn with interest to Machiavelli or to Aristotle. It was provided also that each student should carry on two regional studies, each running through the two years, one dealing with Athens and the other with an American community. This plan was carefully developed by three of the advisers and made a strong appeal both to them and to their colleagues. Had we not been committed to giving the preliminary hypothesis a thorough testing, it is possible that the substitution suggested might have been made.

Two other plans suggest much wider departures from the principle or practice of the Athens-America curriculum. The first of these proposes that instead of taking the different phases of a civilization in succession, one at a time, there should be three different courses running simultaneously. The freshman course as now given devotes approximately the first third of the year to social studies, the second third to literature and the arts, and the last third to religions, science, and philosophy. The proposal is that each of these studies should run through the year, that they be given simultaneously. While it does not change the contents of the course of study, the suggestion obviously involves very radical changes in teaching method.

Still another suggestion brings its attack to bear upon the required curriculum. It objects to the demand that every student, no matter what his special interest or capacity, should follow the same course of study. It proposes, therefore, that each student be allowed at least to start with his own interest, and that the attempt be made to find for each person, from his own starting point, his own way to liberal and general understanding. The plan is strongly favored by at least a small minority of the advisers and is undoubtedly worthy of very careful consideration. It, too, takes us over into serious problems of teaching arrangement and procedure. If a group of teachers should take it as a basis of experimentation, it would furnish very fruitful contrasts with other courses of study.

As one looks back over this account of the deliberations of the advisers, two generalizations seem to emerge. First, with practical unanimity the advisers accept the principle of integration as applied to the course of study of the lower college. They are convinced that the teaching and learning of the two years should conform to a unified and coherent plan. And second, the Athens-America curriculum is one of many possible ways in which unity may be sought. Further experimentation along this line would concern itself (1) with making these suggestions into working plans, and (2) with attempting to determine their relative values.

CHAPTER THIRTEEN

New Directions

THE EXPERIENCE of the Experimental College, fragmentary and often frustrated by its attempt to create new patterns of student life and learning amid a clutter of makeshift facilities and an immense, disorganized, and often hostile undergraduate population, has given powerful warrant to four suggestions for a possible reorganization of the lower college. It will be quickly seen that they are really four different phases of a single point of view.

1. Student social life and education might profit greatly if the freshman and sophomore classes were divided into a number of smaller "colleges" each with its own social identity and social interests.

2. There would be very great gain if the teachers in these smaller colleges could act not only as one body but also as smaller faculties, each working out its own aims and methods in relative independence while considering, together, the educational process as a whole.

3. The Experimental College experience suggests that younger college teachers might in this setting, much more satisfactorily than at present, be trained for the art of teaching.

4. It seems clear that the *cost* of teaching in smaller units and along lines analogous to those adopted by the Experimental College, would at least not be greater than those of the present system.

If we explain each of these statements in turn, the outlines of a working plan will begin to appear.

1. The Undergraduate Community

As one looks with a teacher's eye at the undergraduate life of a university, nothing is more terrifying than its lack of focus. It is not the life of a community, but rather that of a conglomerate of individuals. If that is true, then we are losing the educational value which John Henry Newman regards as basic in all liberal education. The sense of the group to which one belongs, the stirring of its loyalties, the sharing in its creation and support, the enthusiasm of its purposes and its comradeships—these are the stuff out of which the deepest and most vital education is made. But under the social conditions of life in a large university, these values are very largely lost. The students live as scattered individuals, or in accidental and relatively meaningless groups, or in the sorority or fraternity assemblages which are, as such, unrelated or even hostile to the educational purposes of a college. The total effect is—to borrow a phrase from the University Committee of 1924-25—that of a "huge, heterogeneous mass of students and faculty." True, the institution has many eager spirits, both young and old. But there is no focus, no unity, no sense of dominating meaning and purpose and fellowship which might give to intellectual endeavors their proper rounding out into a scheme of rich and happy living.

The needed focus for social and intellectual life might be gained by dividing the lower college into a number of smaller colleges, socially manageable in size. The effect of this policy would be to seize upon the undoubted power and influence of fraternity organization, and to use it in direct contribution to the purposes of the teaching process. If this were done, two results would follow.

First, *every* member of the lower college would be a member of a coherent social group, but without the present brutal separation of "ins" and "outs." Second, the ruling social unit of university life would not be an exclusive and divisive "club" whose internal goals are often hostile to those of the university, but a small and cohesive college, organized and conducted with reference to the essential aims of an institution of learning.

There are many obstacles in the way of carrying out such a program as this. With the present conglomerations of dormitories, boarding houses, fraternity and sorority houses standing in the way, progress would of necessity be slow and difficult. And yet it seems clear that some such venture should be under way, that progress should be made in it as rapidly as possible.

Fifteen or twenty groups of students and teachers, living and working side by side in friendly rivalries and cooperations, might give to an American university what it most sorely needs—a social scheme adapted and adjusted to its teaching aims. Intellectual and social activities might so fuse together that, for practical purposes, one would find no difference between them. In so far as we fall short of that state we fail in the proper social organization of a college community.

2. The Small Faculty

We have said that for educational purposes it is desirable that student groups be small. It seems even more important that the teaching groups, the faculties, be small. The chief tragedy of the piling up of "huge, heterogeneous masses of students and faculty" lies not in the unmanageableness of the student body, serious as that is, but in the unmanageableness of the faculty, with its hundreds or thousands of teachers. Now at this point the experience of the advisers in the Experimental College provides a suggestion which seems well worthy of consideration. The advisers have found themselves in a working group so small that every member has been able to have, in some measure, intellectual as well as personal acquaintance with his colleagues. Each has known what teaching the others were doing and has shared in its planning. The teacher of literature has discussed with the teacher of science how science shall be taught, what books shall be read, what talks shall be given. He has attended the lectures of his colleagues and has discussed them with his students. The effect of this has been to make of the teaching program not a collection of separate activities, but a concerted attempt at definite and unified action. And its effect upon the teacher has been to demand of him that he be not merely a specialized scholar, attending to his own field without regard to what is going on in any other, but a liberally minded man who is concerned with the making and administering of the total education which the students are receiving.

No one can doubt that the achievement of this end is costly in other directions. It is too much to expect of fate that we should get the greatest values without paying for them in the currency of lesser values. But on the other hand, if one really cares for the aims of liberal education, the building up of a liberal outlook and experience among its teachers must be a college's greatest concern. We cannot give liberal education unless the scheme of teaching which attempts it is liberally conceived.

The suggestion, then, which arises out of, or is confirmed by, the experience of the Experimental College is that the general faculty should act not only as a single body, but also in fifteen or twenty separate faculties. Each of these faculties would, under general limitations, have responsibility for its own group of students. Each would devise its own course of study and its own methods of teaching. The different faculties would join together at times to compare teaching methods and results. But the essential gain would be that within each group the scheme of instruction would be unified and coherent. It would be an immediate, living expression of a small group of teachers sufficiently close together to be one in purpose and understanding in the midst of all their differences.

To accomplish this, it would be necessary to keep a proper

balance between two sets of values. First, the faculty must be large enough to give proper representation to different lines of study and research. Literature must have its devotees, and philosophy and science, and the social studies as well. And within these fields there are also separate interests, separate lines of understanding which must be accounted for in a scheme of liberal education. But on the other hand, the group must not be so large as to exceed the limits of easy and informal intellectual acquaintance throughout its membership. It must be a body so unified that all its parts are dealing intelligently with every phase of its activity.

3. The Training of Teachers

The third suggestion is that if small, coherent faculties were established they might serve as training camps for young men and women who are preparing to do college teaching. Everyone knows that at present there are no arrangements for the training of college teachers. Our future professors are rigorously prepared for the activities of scholarship. We demand and require that they "know their subjects." But we do not demand that they understand or master the teaching process, that they know what students need and how their needs can be supplied. And it is obvious that for the purposes of democratic and liberal education this state of affairs is quite intolerable. The activities of liberal teaching must be brought up to the level of an intelligently directed social activity.

Now again, and this time rather by chance than by planning, the Experimental College has hit upon a way in which young teachers might be prepared for their careers. Chiefly for financial reasons, we were forced to take into the faculty a number of young men in their first or second or third year out of college. These men were given the full assignment of individual and group conferences. They had less than the usual share of leading the larger meetings. They found themselves, however, accepted as members of the teaching group in full standing. They shared in all discussions and decisions upon teaching aims, teaching methods, teaching conditions. And the results of the arrangement have been surprisingly satisfactory. These young teachers have done the tutorial work exceedingly well. They have been able to establish sympathetic understanding with freshmen and sophomores and have exerted powerful teaching influence over them. And, on the other hand, they have themselves received valuable training.

If they are planning to be college teachers, there lies before them the double career of scholarship and teaching. It is fair to presume that during the last two years of their undergraduate course they were specializing in some major field. And there are still before them two or three or four years of specialized study on the graduate level. Now from every point of view it would seem to be good training for these young scholar-teachers to devote two or three years between the two "study" periods to association with a group of older men from many departments who are carrying on a common enterprise of instruction. The early teaching responsibility seems to be valuable for them; so too is the close association with older men who are trying to make the many fields of knowledge into one; and the getting of a proper sense of the human opportunities and responsibilities inherent in the life of the teacher is of paramount importance.

4. The Cost of Instruction

Next we want to know if teaching in classes is more or less costly than teaching by individual conference. Our comparison will not be based on the costs of buildings or equipment but simply and solely on the cost of teaching. To put the matter very simply, the question would be, "If you have a fixed number of students to teach, and if the two different systems of teaching are tried, which of the two will require the greater number of teachers?"

For the purposes of our general question of teaching ratios it will be best to deal with a simple situation, one in which we can find liberal colleges not conjoined with other departments as they are of necessity in a university. For this purpose we may take the totals of teachers and students in twenty-six independent colleges from many parts of the country. They are: Mills, Wesleyan, Illinois, Knox, Rockford, Grinnell, Bowdoin, Goucher, Amherst, Mount Holyoke, Smith, Williams, Carleton, Dartmouth, Princeton, Hamilton, Vassar, Wells, Marietta, Reed, Bryn Mawr, Haverford, Swarthmore, Sweet Briar, Beloit, Lawrence.

Now the significant facts for our demonstration can be very simply stated. In the year 1929-30, the total number of students enrolled in these colleges was 20,505. The total number of their full-time teachers was 1,952. Their average teaching ratio is therefore 1 to 10.5. In other words, in these colleges which do their work almost wholly under the class system, one teacher is needed for every ten or eleven students.

But as against this, the teaching ratio in the Experimental College is 1 to 18. The list of advisers is made up in the supposition that each of them will take twelve students under his charge. But the advisers are giving only two-thirds of their time to the college, the other third being reserved for classes "on the Hill" or for graduate study. The full-time ratio is, then, 1 to 18.

But the outcome, as it stands, seems, even to an ardent advocate of individual teaching, too good to be true. How is it possible that by taking students one at a time, instead of in groups of 10 or 50 or 500, one should reduce the teaching ratio, the teaching cost, by about 42 percent?

The answer to that question will be found only when it is remembered that under the class system, as it is ordinarily used, each student has five classes rather than one. In the Experimental College the students are taught in only one subject. Each week the student has one individual conference, one group meeting, and four or five meetings with the class as a whole.

Under the Experimental College plan, a student has six or seven meetings with a teacher each week, while under the class system, he has fifteen or sixteen. And it is this difference which is decisive in the fixing of costs. Whoever wishes, in our colleges, to reduce expenditures for teaching without lessening teaching efficiency would do well to begin at this point.

It still remains that the chief ground for attack upon the traditional arrangement, whereby a student takes five or six courses at a time, is that it is bad educationally, that it is incoherent and chaotic in its teaching effect. But we now see that it is also enormously expensive: As compared with twenty-six representative colleges, the teaching burden in the Experimental College is lower by more than 40 percent.

V.

Epilogue

CHAPTER FOURTEEN

Teachers and Liberal Education

PROBABLY THE MOST profound impression which has been made upon the advisers by their adventure in the teaching of young Americans has been the sense of their own lack of adequate liberal education. This comes from a deep and lively realization of the possibilities and responsibilities of American education, together with the sense of the obstacles that stand in its way.

As one studies the liberal teaching of our colleges, whatever their course of study, whatever their methods of teaching, the most appalling fact about them is the scantness of their educational result, the poverty of their intellectual quality. And there can be no doubt that the deeper reason for this lies in the quality of the teacher himself. We do not teach liberal understanding well because we do not know what it is. Yet, we are very much at home in the field of scholarship.

If a student will limit his interest to some field of intellectual abstraction, we can show him what the human mind has thus far done in that field, can build up in him the proper technique, can equip him, according to his ability, to take his place in the ranks of the craftsmen of that study. And where scholarship is applied to the accomplishment of practical ends, we are again amazingly able, both in achieving results and in training younger men to create still greater ones.

But when men inquire, "What should American life be; toward what ends should it be guided and inspired; in terms of what scheme of ideas and values should it be interpreted and controlled?" the characteristic attitude of many of our greatest scholars is one of despair and utter incapacity. We have many sciences but little wisdom. We have multifarious and accurate information, but we have lost hope of knowing what it means. We are, for the time, beaten in the struggle for liberal education and therefore unable to lead our students into its activities.

Far deeper, then, than any question of curriculum or teaching method or determining conditions is the problem of restoring the courage of Americans, academic or non-academic, to face the essential issues of life. How can it be brought about that the teachers in our colleges and universities shall see themselves, not only as the servants of scholarship, but also, in a far deeper sense, as the creators of the national intelligence? If they lose courage in that endeavor, in whom may we expect to find it? Intelligence, wisdom, sensitiveness, generosity—these cannot be set aside from our planning, to be, as it were, by-products of the scholarly pursuits. They are the ends which all our scholarship and our teaching serve.

Appendixes

The Beginnings of the Experimental College

1. Within the University

In the Annual Report of the University Committee for the year ending November 2, 1925, there appears a record of deliberations and recommendations which, on one side, led to the founding of the Experimental College. Whether to its credit or to its blame, upon that committee must be laid responsibility for initiating the series of events with which the present report deals.

The statement made by the University Committee is an exceedingly interesting and significant document. As their deliberations proceeded the members of the committee were awaiting the selection of a new president of the university and the beginning of a new administration. For this reason, the committee attempted only "to make a rough survey of the field, and on this basis to present queries and suggestions to the faculty and to the new administration." Eighteen meetings were held during the year "in addition to many informal discussions with various members of the faculty, alumni, and students, as well as with the chairmen of a number of university committees."

The report presented three topics for the consideration of the faculty and of the new administration:

First: the relation of the university to the students.

Second: the relation of the university to the alumni.

Third: the relation between the faculty and the regents. It is the first of these which is especially relevant to our story.

THE EXPERIMENTAL COLLEGE

Under the heading, "The Relation of the University to the Students," the committee says:

> From alumni, from graduate students, and from undergraduates, this Committee has received many adverse criticisms of the character of some of the instruction given at the University. More especially is this criticism directed against the large courses of the first two years, in which it is claimed that the students do not get as good teaching as is reasonably possible to give. Is this commonly expressed point of view justified? Obviously the large classes mentioned are not a deliberate choice of any department, but a necessity forced upon us by the ever-increasing number of students and the lack of a proportional increase in staff and buildings. This problem was presented to us from so many sources that a meeting of the Committee was held on April 28, to which the Chairmen of all University departments were invited, to discuss the possibilities of improvement in our teaching method and in our student contacts.

This statement of the committee would seem to make it sufficiently clear that prior to the beginning of the new administration the university community was widely and deeply concerned as to the effectiveness of the teaching in the first two years. And further, the community was evidently of the opinion that here, as well as elsewhere, unsatisfactory teaching arrangements are chiefly due, not to deliberate choice from within, but rather to mechanical and inescapable pressures from without.

In support of its attitude, the committee called attention to a then recent report of the Board of Visitors (to the regents) and commended its references to (1) the need of improvement in instruction, (2) a more adequate advising system, and (3) closer connection between secondary schools and college authorities. It then went on to say, "This admirable study confirms us in the opinion that this University has grown so rapidly as to become somewhat disarticulated." It suggested that it would be well if the members of the faculty would read the annual reports of the Board of Visitors. It mentioned the possibility of the establishment of junior colleges. It recommended the separa-

124

tion of "advising" from "discipline" in the hope that there might be "a Class Adviser appointed for each freshman class and continued as the 'guide, philosopher, and friend' of that class till graduation." It spoke of the need "for the development of intramural sports and games" and for "the creation of better living, social, and recreational conditions for our students." In the latter connection it expressed the hope that the new Memorial Union might be "effective in leavening this huge heterogeneous mass of students and faculty."

"This huge heterogeneous mass of students and faculty"! The university has "become somewhat disarticulated"! Especially is criticism "directed against the large courses of the first two years"! The problem of "teaching methods and student contacts" is "presented to us from so many different sources"! The class adviser should become a "guide, philosopher, and friend"! There is need for "the creation of better living, social, and recreational conditions for our students"! And finally, the members of the faculty should read the annual reports of the Board of Visitors! As one meets these striking phrases one is inclined to rub his eyes to make sure that these are actual words. But there is no mistake; the words are there and they are dated. Nor are they written by outsiders or newcomers. No, these phrases express the well-considered and sober judgment of a responsible faculty committee of the University of Wisconsin of the year 1924-25. It is this committee which, after deliberation with individuals, departments, and committees throughout the university, bluntly called for reconsideration of teaching procedure and social arrangements, with especial reference to the freshman and sophomore years. Criticism of its own procedure was evidently not a new nor an accidental thing in the life of the University of Wisconsin.

But the committee also proceeded from conference and deliberation to recommendation. The second of its three recommendations reads as follows:

II. An All-University Commission of five members (with power to add to their number) shall be appointed from the Faculty by the President to investigate the problems of the articulation of the University in its several parts, but especially to study problems of improvement of instruction and more helpful contacts between students and faculty. The President shall be requested to grant sufficient freedom from other duties to the chairman or other members of this Commission to enable them to pursue these studies.

2. Tentative Steps Outside the University

In the fall of 1924, Mr. Glenn Frank, then editor of the *Century* magazine, published an article by Mr. Alexander Meiklejohn, not then connected with any institution of learning. It was entitled, "A New College, Notes on a Next Step in Higher Education." Conversation between editor and writer concerning the principles and methods of procedure suggested in this article led to consideration of ways and means by which a new experimental project in liberal education might be established. During the winter of 1924-25, in New York, Mr. Frank became a member of a group formed to consider such a project and to take action in furtherance of it if that should seem feasible and advisable. For this committee Mr. Meiklejohn prepared a more specific set of proposals.*

The discussion of these had, however, made little headway when, in the late spring of 1925, Mr. Frank was offered and accepted the presidency of the University of Wisconsin. During that summer the new president suggested to Mr. Meiklejohn that he join the Wisconsin faculty. The two thereupon began considering possible fields of activity in the university. To both men the most attractive possibility was that of transferring to Wisconsin a new educational enterprise by establishing there a small unit of the type they had previously discussed. This plan was long and carefully debated, but in the end it seemed clear that it should not be adopted. Neither of the two was as yet well acquainted with the nature and functioning of a great state university, but

*Published in the *New Republic*, 14 April 1926 under the title "A New College."

both were convinced that, however desirable in itself, the attempt to introduce a novel and relatively independent institution into so complicated a structure would end, and probably end quickly, in disaster. The plan was therefore abandoned, and it was arranged that Mr. Meiklejohn should come to Madison as a teacher of philosophy, beginning his work in February, 1926.

3. The Study Commission

The plan for a "new college," conceived in the East, was dead. In Wisconsin it came to life again but in a different form. In its second birth, it is not a "new" but an "experimental" college. For the proper telling or reading of this story, it is essential that we see and feel the importance of that transformation.

Mr. Frank began his active presidency in September, 1925. Mr. Meiklejohn was to begin his teaching of philosophy in February, 1926. On January 16, 1926, Frank sent a letter to Meiklejohn in which the following startling words appear: "Would you be shocked if I told you that I think I found a way to create and sustain 'an experimental college of liberal arts' inside the university? . . . I am confident that such an experimental laboratory set up inside one of our great universities will more quickly and effectively provide leadership for the whole system of higher education in America than would a separate experimental college. . . . I am concerned that the University of Wisconsin shall provide the first really experimental laboratory of higher education."

If we ask, Why did the new president so quickly reverse an earlier decision; why after four months in the university did he find it ready to give birth and sustenance to a project which before his coming had seemed alien and unwelcome? the answer may be found along two different lines. First, the activities of the University Committee, already mentioned, revealed a demand within the community for fundamental study of its teaching aims and procedures. But side by side with this, there had also appeared an active interest in reconsidering the social phases of student life. This expressed determination to seek new forms of group living which should give promise of genuine educational values was especially seen in the plans for building dormitories for men.

But it was just these two interests which Meiklejohn's projected "new college" in the East had taken as its dominating purposes. If the teaching motive of the earlier, narrower venture could become an item within the larger survey of teaching which the university demanded; if the earlier plans for the forming of a social group should be found to harmonize with those which were to be developed in the new dormitories, then the new college in its changed form might find a useful, a happy place in this self-criticizing university. By entering into the larger scheme of experimentation to which the university was apparently ready to commit itself, the "new college" might be transformed into an experimental college. It was upon the basis of this supposition that the president joined with the University Committee in urging the appointment of an All-University Study Commission.

4. Formal Action

Under its instructions to make a general study of the university, the commission very quickly decided upon the first two years of the College of Letters and Science as the point at which its initial inquiry should be made. It directed Mr. Meiklejohn to prepare general proposals for experimental procedure in those two years along the lines of his earlier, published suggestions. These proposals, after being subjected to sharp and lively criticisms, were made into a concrete plan by a subcommittee of Dean Sellery and Mr. Meiklejohn, and this plan was approved. It was recommended to the Faculty of Letters and Science, first in a general report, and next as a scheme of concrete legislation. This scheme was amended in two particulars by the Faculty of Letters and Science, and, being then adopted on May 26, 1926, was in turn approved by the University Faculty and by the Board of Regents. The Experimental College thus came into legal being.

Since action had been taken late in the academic year, it seemed impossible to make necessary preparations in time for the opening of the college in September, 1926. Mr. Meiklejohn was appointed chairman of the college with instructions to select a faculty and to invite the registration of students. These arrangements were made during the year 1926-27, and in September, 1927, the college began its work.

Assignments for the Class Leaving the College in June, 1932

Freshman Year
First Year Book List
1930-31

The following books are in the freshman study rooms (fellow's suite) in La Follette House:

Agard, W.R., *The Greek Tradition in Sculpture*
Anderson, W.J., *The Architecture of Greece and Rome*
Aristophanes, *The Frogs and Other Plays; Plays* (Loeb Classical Library); *The Clouds*
Aristotle, *Aristotle on the Art of Poetry; De Partibus Animalium; Politics; Oeconomica; Nicomachean Ethics*
Atherton, G., *The Immortal Marriage*
Bakewell, *Sourcebook of Ancient Philosophy*
Barker, Ernest, *Greek Political Theory*
Bell, Clive, *Art; Civilization*
Bonner, R.J., *Lawyers and Litigants in Ancient Athens*
Botsford, G.W., *Hellenic Civilization*
Burnet, John, *Early Greek Philosophy*
Bury, J.B., *A History of Greece to the Death of Alexander the Great*
Calhoun, G.M., *The Business Life of Ancient Athens; The Growth of Criminal Law in Ancient Greece*
Cambridge Ancient History (ed. by J.B. Bury and others)
Carpenter, R., *Esthetic Basis of Greek Art*
Carritt, E.F., *The Theory of Beauty*
Collignon, *Le Parthenon* (pictures)
Croiset, *Aristophanes, and the Political Parties in Athens*

Class Assignments

Cushman, *Beginners' History of Philosophy*

Davis, W.S., *A Day in Old Athens; A Victor of Salamis*

Demosthenes, *The Crown, the Philippics, and Ten Other Orations.*

Dickinson, G.L., *The Greek View of Life*

Epictetus, *Moral Discourses*

Euripides, *Alcestis; The Bacchae; Hippolytus; Iphigenia; Tragedies; Trojan Women*

Fowler, *A Handbook of Greek Archeology*

Fox, *Greek and Roman Mythology*

Freeman, K.J., *Schools of Hellas*

Galen, *Galen on the Natural Faculties*

Gardner, E.A., *Ancient Athens; Six Greek Sculptors*

Glaspell, Susan, *The Road to the Temple*

Glotz, Gustave, *Ancient Greece at Work; Greek City*

Greenidge, A.H.J., *A Handbook of Greek Constitutional History*

Grundy, G.B. (ed.), *Murray's Small Classical Atlas*

Gulick, C.B., *The Life of the Ancient Greeks*

Harrison, Jane, *Ancient Art and Ritual*

Heath, Sir Thomas, *A History of Greek Mathematics*

Heiberg, J.L., *Mathematics and Physical Science in Classical Antiquity*

Herodotus, *History*

Hesiod, *Poems and Fragments*

Hippocrates, *Works*

Holdt, Hans, *Picturesque Greece* (pictures)

Homer, *Iliad; Odyssey*

Horton, *Home of Nymphs and Vampires*

Howe, George (ed.), *Greek Literature in Translation*

Hutchinson, W.M.L.,*The Muses' Pageant* (mythology)

Hyde, William DeWitt, *The Five Great Philosophies of Life*

Jebb, *Attic Orators*

Laistner, M.L.W. (ed. and tr.), *Greek Economics*

Lippmann, Walter, *Public Opinion*

Livingstone, R.W. (ed.), *The Legacy of Greece; The Greek Genius and Its Meaning to Us*

Lucian, *Works*

131

Mackail, J.W., *Select Epigrams from the Greek Anthology*
Marshall, F.H., *Discovery in Greek Lands*
Mears, *Greece Today*
Mitchison, Naomi, *Cloud Cuckoo Land*
Moore, C.H., *The Religious Thought of Greeks*
Murray, Gilbert, *A History of Ancient Greek Literature;
Euripides and His Age; Five Stages of Greek Religion;
Tradition and Progress*
Myres, J.L., *The Political Ideas of the Greeks*
Norwood, Gilbert, *Greek Tragedy*
Pindar, *Odes*
Plato, *Dialogues*
Plutarch, *Lives* ("Dryden Plutarch," revised by A.H.
Clough); *Six Lives* (Perrin)
Poulsen, Frederik, *Delphi*
Pouten, *Grieschen Landschaften*
Prall, *Aesthetic Judgment*
Richter, G., *The Sculpture and Sculptors of Ancient Greece*
Robin, L., *Greek Thought*
Ross, W.D., *Aristotle*
Sargent, *Greek Athletics*
Savage, C.A., *The Athenian Family*
Scoon, Robert, *Greek Philosophy before Plato*
Sheppard, *Greek Tragedy*
Showerman, G. (ed.), *Century Readings in Ancient Classical
Literature*
Sophocles, *Antigone*
Stage, W.T., *A Critical History of Greek Philosophy*
Swindler, M.H., *Ancient Painting*
Symonds, J.A., *Studies of the Greek Poets*
Taylor, H.O., *Greek Biology and Medicine*
Thucydides, *Peloponnesian War*
Toynbee, A.J., *Greek Civilization and Character; The
Tragedy of Greece*
University Prints—*Greek and Roman Sculpture* (pictures);
European Architecture
Verrall, *Euripides, the Rationalist*
Vinogradov, P., *Outlines of Historical Jurisprudence; The*

Jurisprudence of the Greek City
Warren, H.L., *The Foundations of Classic Architecture*
Xenophon, *Hellenica*, Vol. I
Zielinski, *The Religion of Ancient Greece*
Zimmern, *The Greek Commonwealth; Solon and Croesus*

Freshman Assignments*
September 24, 1930

Each student should have for use the following books:

Herodotus' *History*; Thucydides' *History*; Edman: *The Works of Plato*; Plays of Aeschylus; Sophocles' *Antigone, Oedipus the King*; *Media, Alcestis,* and *Trojan Women* of Euripides; *Clouds,* and *Knights* of Aristophanes; Plato's *Republic; The Legacy of Greece*; Botsford's *Hellenic History*; Zimmern's *The Greek Commonwealth*; Homer's *Iliad* or *Odyssey.*

For the first paper, due Saturday noon, October 4, make a careful study of the Funeral Speech of Pericles. Analyze the meaning of the various points and the way in which they are woven together. Give your own reactions to each part and to the speech as a whole.

The following meetings will be held at 9 A.M. in the New Soils Building:

Thursday, September 25, discussion of the assignment.
Saturday, September 27, Mr. Bogholt on the Apology of Socrates.
Tuesday, September 30, Mr. Agard on the Geography of Greece.
Thursday, October 2, Mr. Agard on Greek Life as Seen in Greek Art.
Saturday, October 4, Mr. Agard on the Greek Language.

---

*Because many of the books that were used in the Experimental College are now either out of print or available only in new editions, we have deleted most of the weekly reading assignments from this edition of *The Experimental College.*

THE EXPERIMENTAL COLLEGE

October 6, 1930

The study of human relations in fifth-century Athens may well begin with Athenian wars. For the next two or three weeks we shall consider Athens's relations to other states.

Reading:

Herodotus' *History.*
Thucydides' *History of the Peloponnesian War.*
You may find it desirable to begin your acquaintance with Thucydides by reading some selected passages which will introduce you to his character and indicate the structure of his story.

Some reading on modern warfare:

B. Russell, *Why Men Fight*; Angell, *The Great Illusion*; Remarque, *All Quiet on the Western Front*; Zweig, *The Case of Sergeant Grischa*; Zola, *La Débâcle*; Reynal, *The Unknown Warrior*; Tolstoi, *War and Peace*; Sherriff, *Journey's End*; Anderson and Stallings, *What Price Glory?* Robert Graves, *Good-bye to All That*; Sassoon, *Memoirs of an Infantry Officer*; The London Naval Conference: news accounts and editorial comments. .

Paper, due October 20:

Describe the policy and activities of Athens in her foreign affairs under (1) Themistocles, (2) Pericles, and (3) Alcibiades.

Indicate in your study what you find to admire or criticize in her policy and its execution. A map should illustrate and accompany the paper. Each student may bring a notebook, along with the drafts of his map and paper, to conferences with his adviser.

Talks:

Tuesday, October 7, at 9 o'clock, Mr. Meiklejohn will speak to the class about the plan of work for the year and particularly the plan for the fall term.

Thursday, October 9, at 9·o'clock, Mr. Sharp will discuss some problems raised by the events described in the histories of Herodotus and Thucydides.

October 20, 1930

In our study of Greek society we find men holding conflicting opinions in regard to matters of public policy. Both parties to a controversy are observed to claim "right" or "justice" in support of their views. A question naturally arises as to the meaning and validity of these terms. The reading and discussion during the coming week will be concerned mainly with this question.

Paper, due October 27:

Thucydides' *History of the Peloponnesian War*:
   Plataean Eipsode
   Melian Episode
   Mitylenian Episode
The student is requested to take *one* of the above episodes and examine it in light of the week's reading and discussion. Is there a "right" involved in the situation? If not, give the basis for your judgment. If so, how do you justify your opinion?

Talks:

Tuesday, October 21, Professor McGilvary of the University Department of Philosophy.
Thursday, October 23, Professor Otto of the University Department of Philosophy.
Friday, October 24, Mr. Bogholt will lead the discussion.
Saturday, October 25, Mr. Bogholt will lead the discussion.

October 27, 1930

It seems desirable to consider next the way in which the Athenians conducted their daily life, earned their living, and governed themselves. We shall find that their daily activities raised troublesome problems, comparable to the problem of war; and we shall find, again, that Plato has something to say about these problems. In order to understand the life of the city, we shall concentrate for the next four or five weeks on Zimmern's *Greek Commonwealth*. At the same time, it seems desirable that we should be doing a first reading of Plato's *Republic* in preparation for a period devoted to a discussion of Plato's ideal city. Throughout the period we shall of course be interested in discovering whether the experience of Athens and the suggestions of Plato throw any light on our contemporary situation.

The first topic for investigation and discussion is *the creation of wealth.*

For a modern book comparable to *The Greek Commonwealth*, see Lynd, *Middletown*.

Paper, due November 3:

"Ways of Earning a Living in Pericles' Athens"

Talks:

Tuesday, October 28, and Thursday, October 30, there will be opportunities for the class to discuss questions raised by the assignment, with Mr. Koch or Mr. Sharp or both.

November 1, 1930
Conflicts About Wealth

Reading:

Zimmern, *The Greek Commonwealth*

See also:

Plutarch, *Life of Solon; Life of Pericles*
Aristophanes, Comedies
The Old Oligarch (in pamphlet form; and reprinted in Botsford and Sihler, *Hellenic Civilization*)
Croiset, *Aristophanes and the Political Parties in Athens*
Aristotle's *Politics*
Compare any relevant modern material like *The Commu-*

ist Manifesto; R.H. Tawney, *The Acquisitive Society*; Andrew Carnegie's *Autobiography*; The writings of Henry Ford.

Paper, due November 10:

Describe the conflict about wealth with which Solon had to deal. What did Solon do about this conflict? Did any similar conflict face Pericles? Do you find any similar conflict today? If so, what is your opinion and your own attitude toward it?

Talks:

Tuesday, November 4, and Thursday, November 6, there will be opportunities for the class to discuss questions raised by the assignment, with Mr. Koch or Mr. Sharp or both.

November 10, 1930
Functions and Structure of Government

During this period the situation in Athens should be compared with the situation in Sparta and particularly with the ideal scheme described in Plato's *Republic*. It seems likely that "democratic" Athens is being criticized and "aristocratic" Sparta qualifiedly approved in the *Republic*. If we can develop a reasonably clear understanding of the government of both Athens and Sparta, we shall, among other things, be better prepared to understand and discuss Plato's philosophy of government.

We have now become acquainted with a good deal of the literature dealing with the economic and political life of Athens and Sparta; and it therefore seems unnecessary to set forth an extended list of readings.

A suggested modern book is A.P. Herring, *Group Representation Before Congress*.

Paper, due November 17:

What work did the governing bodies of Athens do, and how were they organized under Cleisthenes? Compare the constitution under Pericles. Compare the constitution of

Sparta. Discuss the merits and defects of each constitution.

Talks:

There will be meetings of the class at 9 o'clock on Tuesday and Thursday, November 11 and 13.

November 17-December 1, 1930
Democracy

During the next two weeks we shall have an opportunity to go over all the material which we have thus far been studying; and to organize and enrich our knowledge and understanding of the social, economic, and political life of Athens and the modern world. There will be an opportunity, for example, to consider the relationship of such institutions as the family, slavery, and the empire to the other institutions and events which we have been studying. There will also be an opportunity for each of us to think further about any special phase of Athenian life which has been of particular interest and to discuss the relationship of this phase of life to other aspects of Athens and the modern world. To prevent reading and discussion from becoming utterly formless, there will be a paper on the rather large subject, "Democracy."

Suggested Readings:

Compare books on contemporary conditions. Suggested readings on conditions at other periods than the fifth century are:

Rostovtzeff, *Social and Economic History of the Roman Empire*; G. B. Shaw, *The Intelligent Woman's Guide to Socialism and Capitalism*; Wallas, *The Great Society, Human Nature in Politics*; Santayana, *Character and Opinion in the United States*; Unemployment Conference Committee (Herbert Hoover, Chairman) *Recent Economic Changes in the United States*; Lippmann, *Public Opinion, The Phantom Public*; Frank Kent, *The Great Game of Politics*

138

Paper, due December 1:

What do you mean by democracy—social, economic, political? Consider the social, economic, and political life of Athens: Was Athens democratic in the sense in which you use the term?

Meetings:

There will be meetings on Tuesday and Thursday mornings at 9 o'clock unless announcements to the contrary are made; and other meetings will probably be held and announced on the bulletin board.

December, 1930

The chief desire of the advisers for the period beginning Tuesday, December 2, is that the students should begin a sympathetic and thorough study of the *Republic* as a statement of Plato's Utopia. In connection with this study of the *Republic*, students are asked to read *Humanity Uprooted* by Maurice Hindus.

Suggested Readings:

Aristotle, *Politics*; Mumford, *Story of Utopias*; Bacon, *New Atlantis*; More, *Utopia*; Bellamy, *Looking Backward*; Butler, *Erewhon*; Wells, *Men Like Gods*; Russell, *The National Being*; Dewey, *Impressions of Soviet Russia*.

The paper for the period should be handed in not later than December 19. The student may choose any topic he wishes bearing on Plato's *Republic*.

During the period there will be talks by advisers and outside lecturers on the *Republic* and on various phases of social planning.

January 6–February 2, 1931
Greek Art

I. *General Plan*: Use your eyes: look critically at room decorations, dress, automobiles, buildings, sculpture, paintings, etc. Visit the exhibitions in the union and the university library. Get similarly acquainted with Greek art—costumes, objects of everyday use, and the buildings, sculpture, and vases suggested below. First, look at pictures of them, sketch them, remember them. Regarding each object, ask yourself: Do I like this or not? Why? Find out all you can about it. Then ask yourself questions like these:

1. What sort of people were the artists in Athens? Why were they artists? Under what conditions did they work? What was their function considered to be? Their relationship to other members of the community?

2. How far did they follow artistic traditions? Did they tend to maintain traditional molds or invent new ones? (Cf. with Greek drama.)

3. In what respects did Greek art express changing Greek social standards and national ideals? What was the relation between art and athletics? art and government? art and religion? art and morals?

4. How do you respond emotionally and intellectually to Greek art? Does it seem to you "cold"?

5. What values of texture do you find in Greek art? color and modeling? line, pattern, and mass? Distinguish these values in various buildings, statues, and paintings.

6. Compare the temple at Corinth, the Parthenon, and the Temple of Zeus Olympius at Athens with respect to artistic conception and technique. Also the Charioteer of Delphi, the Parthenon "Theseus" and the Hermes of Praxiteles. Also vases by Execias, Euphronius, and Meidias. Does the evolution imply aesthetic progress?

7. What are the limitations of Greek art?

8. What survivals of Greek art do you find in contemporary life? Are they important? Especially, what ones do you find in Madison? (Use your sketchbook.) Which is closer to the Greek—the Nashville Parthenon or a prairie home by Frank Lloyd Wright? the Lincoln Memorial or the Shelton Hotel?

9. To what degree are we justified in copying or adapting

Greek art today? Is it in any way expressive of contemporary culture?

10. What regional art have we developed in America which is an adequate expression of local character?

11. By what standards do you judge a work of art? Compare the Parthenon, Chartres Cathedral, the Shelton Hotel, N.Y. Compare the Apollo of Olympia, Donatello's St. George, Bourdelle's Mickiewicz. Compare Euphronius' Munich cup drawings, Botticelli's Primavera, Picasso's drawings.

12. Define art. What is it good for?

13. Compare the function and value of art in Greek and American life. Also, if you are interested, continue the comparison in medieval France, Renaissance Italy, contemporary Russia.

II. *Objects for Special Study—Buildings*: Parthenon, Erechtheum, "Theseum," Temple of Zeus Olympius at Athens, Theatre at Epidaurus. *Sculpture*: On the temples of Aphaia at Aegina, of Zeus at Olympia, Parthenon, Mausoleum at Halicarnassus; great altar of Pergamon. Also the Charioteer of Delphi, Ludovisi Throne, Victory by Paeonius, Hermes by Praxiteles, Athenian tombstones of Dexileos and Hegeso, Agias by Lysippus, Aphrodite of Melos, Victory of Samothrace. *Vases*: A few by Execias, Euphronius, Brygus, Meidias.

III. *Books*:

1. For pictures: *Picturesque Greece*; Richter, *Sculpture and Sculptors of the Greeks*; Swindler, *Ancient Painting*.

2. General Reference: Fowler and Wheeler, *Greek Archaeology*; E. Faure, *History of Art* (Vol. I); H. S. Jones, *Ancient Writers on Greek Sculpture*.

3. Architecture: Anderson, Spiers and Dinsmoor, *Architecture of Ancient Greece*; Warren, *Foundations of Classic Architecture*; Marquand, *Greek Architecture* (details); E. Gardner, *Ancient Athens*; Weller, *Athens and Its Monuments*;

Collignon, *Le Parthenon*; Robertson, *Greek and Roman Architecture*.

4. Sculpture: Richter, *Sculpture and Sculptors of the Greeks*; E. Gardner, *Handbook of Greek Sculpture, Six Greek Sculptors*; von Mach, *Handbook of Greek Sculpture*, Collignon, *La Sculpture Grecque*; Dickens, *Hellenistic Sculpture*; Poulsen, *Delphi*; Agard, *The Greek Tradition in Sculpture*; Lawrence, *Classical Sculpture*.

5. Vases: Pfuhl, *Masterpieces of Greek Drawing and Painting*; Buscher, *Greek Vase Painting*; M. H. Swindler, *Ancient Painting*.

6. Interpretation: Plato, *Republic* (Books 3 and 10), *Phaedrus, Laws* (Book 2); *Walter Pater, Greek Art*; G. L. Dickinson, *Greek View of Life*; P. Gardner, *Principles of Greek Art*; R. Carpenter, *Esthetic Basis of Greek Art*; C. Bell, *Art*; Santayana, *Reason in Art*; Havelock Ellis, *The Dance of Life*; Carritt, *The Theory of Beauty*; Benvenuto Cellini, *Autobiography*; Leonardo da Vinci, *Notebooks*; Homer Saint-Gaudens, *Augustus Saint-Gaudens*.

7. Modern implications: S. Cheney, *Primer of Modern Art*; E. Faure, *History of Art* (Vol. IV); L. Mumford, *Sticks and Stones*; S. Cheney, *The New World Architecture*; Edgell, *American Architecture of Today*; Taut, *Modern Architecture*, LeCorbusier, *Towards a New Architecture*; S. Casson, *Some Modern Sculptors, Twentieth Century Sculptors*; L. Taft, *Modern Tendencies in Sculpture*; A. M. Rindge, *Sculpture*; C. Post, *History of European and American Sculpture*; F. J. Mather, *Modern Paintings*; S. LaFollette, *Art in America*. Also get acquainted with the art magazines in the university library periodical room, especially *The Arts, Creative Art, Art Digest, Architectural Record, Architectural Forum*.

IV. *Talks*: There will be the following talks:
January 6, "What is the use of architecture?"
January 8, "Greek architecture."
January 20, "What is the use of sculpture?"
January 22, "Greek sculpture."
January 27, "Greek painting."

V. *Conferences*: Mr. Agard will meet students interested in discussion in the Soils Building at 9 o'clock on the following mornings: January 7, January 15, January 21, and January 29. Tentative subjects for discussion are: Plato's conception of art, art and morality, art as "significant form," art in America.

VI. *Assignments*: During this period compare Greek and modern art in detail. It is especially desirable that each student try his hand at some artistic expression: Use a sketchbook; take photographs of architecture and sculpture hereabouts; try modeling clay. Visit Mr. Topchevsky's studio—work with him; get acquainted with what he is doing and how he is doing it; find out what your artistic ability is. Examples of your own craftsmanship and a paper on some phase of the function and value of art will be due February 2.

Freshman Literature Assignment
February 3-23, 1931

Students are advised to read plays aloud together and to keep a notebook recording their reaction to the reading. Contrast the spirit and technique of Greek and modern literature.

Required Reading:
1. Either the *Iliad* or the *Odyssey*.
2. Poems by Sappho; Mackail, *Select Epigrams from the Greek Anthology*; Aeschylus, *Agamemnon, Libation Bearers, Eumenides, Prometheus*; Sophocles, *Antigone, Oedipus the King, Oedipus at Colonus*; Euripides, *Bacchae, Hippolytus, Trojan Women, Alcestis, Electra*; Aristophanes, *Frogs, Birds, Clouds, Lysistrata*; Aristotle, *Poetics*; Plato, *Symposium, Phaedrus*.

Suggested Reading:
1. Other plays by the four Greek dramatists, by Shakespeare, Ibsen, Chekhov, O'Neill, or any other good playwright.

2. Any of the following books about Greek literature and drama: F. L. Lucas, *Tragedy*; Norwood, *Greek Tragedy*; Flickinger, *The Greek Theatre and Its Drama*; J. Harrison, *Ancient Art and Ritual*; Symonds, *The Greek Poets*; G. Murray, *The Rise of the Greek Epic*; D. M. Robinson, *Sappho and Her Influence*; J. W. Mackail, *Lectures on Greek Poetry*; M. Croiset, *Aristophanes and the Political Parties in Athens*.

3. It would be well to read some good modern novel as an interesting contrast to the narratives of Homer.

Written Assignment:

An informal notebook or diary of your reading in which you may discuss points that interest, please, or puzzle you; include quotations. Here are a few suggestions of things that you might make note of. Which books were your favorites? Which did you dislike and why? What differences or resemblances did you notice between the various Greeks, between the moderns, between the Greeks and the moderns? How much do you think you lost of the Greeks and the Elizabethans by the fact that their writings are inevitably reflections of a way of life different in many respects from ours? How much of your interest and pleasure in reading was derived from the characters and ideas presented? How much from the beauty and power of the ordering and writing? How clearly can you distinguish these two kinds of satisfaction? Do they really exist as distinct from each other?

Don't let consideration of these questions cramp your style. They are merely tentative suggestions to get you started. This notebook should be brought to the personal conferences and will be handed in to the adviser on February 23.

Talks for the Period:

Tuesday, February 3, "An Approach to Poetry," Mr. Beecher.

Thursday, February 5, "An Analysis of the Agamemnon," Mr. Agard.

Tuesday, February 10, "A New 'House of Atreus,'" Mr. Beecher.

Thursday, February 12, "The Three Greek Tragedians,"
Mr. Agard.

Tuesday, February 17, "Homer," Mr. Winspear.

Thursday, February 19, "Aristophanes," Mr. Winspear.

Discussion Meetings:

Discussion meetings will be held in the New Soils Building
at 9 o'clock every Wednesday and Friday.

February 23-March 2, 1931

So far we have been making a phase-by-phase study of the
various activities of Athens. But there is an important
question, as yet only suggested, which should be faced
squarely before the end of this year: To what extent were
these different activities interrelated in the experience of the
individuals and of the community as a whole? We must try to
find out what sort of values the Athenians prized most and
how they sought to realize them. In other words, what is the
total picture of their community life, and how far did they
succeed in creating what may be considered a great civilization?

In order to raise these problems, the advisers will lead the
following class discussions:

Tuesday, February 24, "Socrates and Civilization," Mr.
Meiklejohn.

Wednesday, February 25, "What Was Fun for a Greek?"
Mr. Agard.

Thursday, February 26, subject to be announced, Mr.
Powell.

Friday, February 27, subject to be announced, Mr. Havighurst.

March 2-16, 1931
Religion Period

Reading:

Every student is asked to read Zielinski—*The Religion of
Ancient Greece.*

Library Facilities:

It has been arranged that some of the freshman advisers will leave their offices on the second floor of La Follette House unlocked. These rooms are to be considered a part of the library and may be used for reading when the library is filled, provided they are not already in use by advisers for study or conference.

Paper, due March 16:

What things, in your judgment, does religion do for men? How well did the Greek religion do these things for the Athenians of Pericles' time?

Meetings:

Saturday, February 28, 9 o'clock, Professor A. E. Haydon of the University of Chicago.

Monday, March 2, 9 o'clock, Professor Haydon.

Tuesday, March 3, 9 o'clock, Dr. Meiklejohn.

Wednesday, March 4, 9 o'clock, "Humanism," Mr. Hart.

Thursday, March 5, 9 o'clock, "The Mysteries," Mr. Havighurst.

Friday, March 6, 9 o'clock, Discussion of Zielinski's book, Mr. Agard.

Tuesday, March 10, 9 o'clock, "A Survey of Religion in Fifth-Century Athens," Mr. Havighurst.

Wednesday, March 11, 9 o'clock, "Judaism versus Hellenism," Mr. Havighurst.

March 16-30, 1931
Science Period

This period will be devoted to a study of the answers found by the Greeks during the sixth and fifth centuries to the fundamental questions which science has always been asking about the nature of the world. Some attention will also be devoted to tracing out the relationship between modern scientific concepts and those of the Greeks.

The talks which will be given during the period are designed to help you to understand the material which you read, some of which may prove rather difficult, and also to relate the Greek science with modern science, which the reading assignment does not do. It is advisable that you complete some of the reading assignment which accompanies a given talk before listening to that talk.

The schedule of talks and reading assignments is as follows:

Tuesday, March 17—9 o'clock: "Introduction to the Science and Philosophy Periods," Dr. Meiklejohn.

Wednesday, March 18: "The Rise of a Scientific Interpretation of the World Among the Greeks," Mr. Havighurst.

Thursday, March 19: "The Milesians," Mr. Havighurst.

Friday, March 20: "Heraclitus and Parmenides," Mr. Havighurst.

Tuesday, March 24: "The Pluralists," Mr. Havighurst.

Wednesday, March 25: "The Pythagoreans," Mr. Havighurst.

Thursday, March 26: "Squaring the Circle," Mr. Havighurst.

Friday, March 27: "Greek Medicine," Mr. Norman Cameron.

Paper, due March 30:

Subject may be chosen from the following:

1. Describe and criticize from the viewpoint of your own knowledge the answers of the sixth- and fifth-century Greeks to one of the following questions: What is Being? What is Becoming? What is the relation between the One and the Many?

2. Describe the answers to the above questions given by one of the scientists of the sixth and fifth centuries and criticize it from the point of view of the knowledge which you think he might have possessed.

3. Describe the conflict between Parmenides and Heraclitus and criticize their answers to the question in dispute.

R. J. Havighurst.

THE EXPERIMENTAL COLLEGE

March 30-May 4, 1931
Philosophy Period

During the troublous times of external wars and internal party strife which followed the death of Pericles, the cultivated youth of Greece began to ask questions of one another—to ask about themselves and about the activities they were supposed to carry on. There arose critical discussions of all sorts of fields—morals, manners, military tactics, politics, poetry, grammar, and more besides—in terms of the *ideas* or concepts or definitions which those activities involve; and some men, whom we should call philosophers in a stricter sense, turned to critical discussion of the ideas involved in the very practice of critical discussion. They asked one another about the nature of Reason, and whether Parmenides had the right of it in exalting Reason over Sense-perception. They asked whether the things revealed by this Reason were more real than those revealed by perception, what *reality* meant, then, and whether it didn't all smack of irreligion. They asked how one concept could stand for many cases, or one Truth arise among many men, when clearly what is sensed depends upon the nature of the man who senses it, and the smell of Truth upon whose nose detects it.

They asked their fathers, and their uncles, the dignified Strategoi, What Duty ever did for them, that they should do so much for her: Weren't the unjust more likely than the just to win power and pleasure? And their uncles, who had power but no joy of it—you know the kind of life those Strategoi led—assured the young men that not pleasure, but Wisdom, was the aim of life. So the young men turned to men who professed to teach Wisdom and Virtue: Protagoras of Abdera, and Gorgias of Leontini, and Hippias of Elis, and Prodicus of Ceos; but Socrates was forever interrupting with his questions, whether Virtue could be taught, even if you could decide what it was; or was it the same as Wisdom? One of these young men, pondering these questions with unusual boldness and persistence, became a great philosopher: Plato, the pupil of Socrates and the teacher of Aristotle.

148

Now, the Greeks were living in a democracy where mass-opinion was powerful, and where most people thought in confused, superstitious ways, and believed what they read in the papers, and flocked to teachers of Personality and Public Speaking, and paid great tribute to athletes. So the thoughtful ones found it important to discover what good Thinking was, where Reality lay, what kind of Happiness to aim for, and whether Man was really the measure of all things.

What kind of democracy do you find yourself living in? If it seems somewhat like theirs, wouldn't you expect to find their questions somewhat vital for yourself? I don't insist; I only want to suggest that in reading Plato we are entering, not a perfumed study, but the society of a man who fought to understand and fought to criticize his own age, and whose voice has the unique merit of sounding contemporary in every age.

John W. Powell.

For the next five weeks our discussion will center about the problems suggested: the use of reason, the nature of the concepts it works with, the sort of reality it discloses; the value of pleasure; and the general sophistic position as to the relativity of all judgments of fact and of value. There will be class discussions on Tuesday, Wednesday, Thursday, Friday of each week; and three short papers will be asked of each student. The effort will be rather to get the problems clearly stated than definitively answered.

Papers will be due as follows:

Monday, April 6: Plato's "Analogy of the Cave": A brief discussion of its meaning and implications.

Monday, April 20: Pleasure as the aim of life: your own views in the light of Plato's *Protagoras*; *Theaetetus*; *Republic*, Bks. I and II, to the end of the argument on justice, and Bk. IX. *Philebus* and *Gorgias* are recommended also.

Monday, May 4: State the issue between Plato and the Sophists as to Relativity, giving careful textual references on both sides. Give your own argument on the question.

Protagoras; *Theaetetus*; *Symposium*; *Phaedrus*; *Phaedo*, *Meno*, and especially *Gorgias* are recommended also. The *Republic* is rich in material.

———————

Appended is a list of modern contributors to the Platonic discussions—not very many—nor always the best, but worth attention:

Berkeley, *Principles of Human Knowledge*; Descartes, *Discourse on Method; Meditations*; Dewey, *The Quest for Certainty*; William James, *The Philosophy of William James; The Will to Believe*; Jeans, *The Mysterious Universe*; Pearson, *The Grammar of Science*; Santayana, *The Realm of Essence; Dialogues in Limbo*.

April 24, 1931

From May 4 to June 5, each student will work on a special phase of Greek life which especially interests him, and the students working in the same general field will meet as a group to discuss the interrelationships between their subjects of research.

The final paper will be due Friday noon, June 5. Final conferences will be held June 6-13. The special adviser and one other adviser will confer with each student on the results of his research.

Sophomore Year
Book List for Introductory Study
of Physical Science

The World-Picture of Modern Science:

Andrade, *The Mechanism of Nature*
Birkhoff, *The Origin, Nature, and Influence of Relativity*
Bragg, W. H., *Concerning the Nature of Things*
Darrow, *The New World of Physical Discovery*
Eddington, *The Nature of the Physical World, Stars and Atoms*

Einstein, *Relativity*
Erwin, *The Universe and the Atom*
Jeans, *The Universe Around Us; The Mysterious Universe.*
Joly, *The Birth-Time of the World*
Lodge, *Atoms and Rays*
Luckiesch, *Foundations of the Universe*
Millikan, *The Electron*
Mills, *Within the Atom; The Realities of Modern Science*
Russell, B., *The A B C of Relativity*
Shapley, *Flights from Chaos*
Stetson, *Man and the Stars*
Sullivan, J. W. N., *Bases of Modern Science*
                          Atoms and Electrons
Whetham, *Matter and Change*

History of Physical Science:

Buckley, *History of Physics*
Crew, *The Rise of Modern Physics*
Knickerbocker, *Classics of Modern Science*
Sedgwick and Tyler, *A Short History of Science*
Shapley and Howarth, *A Source-Book in Astronomy*
Whetham, *Cambridge Readings in the Literature of Science*

Scientific Method:

Bacon, Francis, *Novum Organum*
Bridgman, *The Logic of Modern Physics*
Burtt, *Metaphysical Foundations of Modern Science*
Descartes, *Discourse on Method*
Mach, *Analysis of the Sensations*
              The Science of Mechanics
Poincare, *Foundations of Science*
Ritchie, A.D., *Scientific Method*
Thomson, J.A., *Introduction to Science*
Whetham, *The Foundations of Science*
Whewell, *Philosophy of the Inductive Sciences*
Whitehead, *Science and the Modern World*
Wolf, A., *Essentials of Scientific Method*

Textbooks:

Black and Davis, *Practical Physics*
Caven, *Atoms and Molecules*
Cranston, *The Structure of Matter*
Duff, *Text-book of Physics*
Kimball, *College Physics*
Knowlton, *Physics for College Students*
Millikan, Gale, and Edwards, *A First Course in Physics*
Saunders, *Survey of Physics*
Sheldon, Kent, Paton, Miller, *Physics for Colleges*
Smith, A. W., *Elements of Physics*
Spinney, *A Textbook of Physics*
Weld and Palmer, *Textbook of Modern Physics*

Sophomore Assignments
September 23-October 31, 1931
Physical Science Period

Meetings:

To be held every day at 10 o'clock unless notice is given to the contrary.

Introduction:

The first few days will be given to a consideraton of world-pictures in general and of the new scientific world-picture in particular. The reading assignment is as follows:

Bible—Genesis, Chs. 1 and 2; Psalms 8, 19, 33, 90, 104, 121, 139, 148; Isaiah, Ch. 40, v. 12-24, Ch. 42, v. 5-8; Job, Ch. 38, v. 1-34.
Havighurst, *Introduction to Physical Science*, Ch. 1.

Laboratory Work:

During the month of October each student may spend two hours a day, five days a week in the physics laboratory. The directions for the experimental work are to be found in the textbook. The daily meetings will be devoted to discussion of the laboratory work and of the reading in the textbook.

Reading:

Havighurst, *Introduction to Physical Science*, will be used for laboratory work and for daily discussions.

Every student is asked to read the following books, which may be purchased in cheap editions or borrowed from the university library: Stuart Chase, *Men and Machines*; de Kruif, *Microbe Hunters*.

Advisers will suggest further reading, when it is desired, from the Science Bibliography.

Papers:

October   3—The history of your own world-picture *or* What element of the modern scientific world-picture interests you most?

October 19—The method of science as illustrated in the development of the kinetic-molecular theory.

October 26—The physical reality of atoms and molecules.

November 2—What do we mean by a "true theory" in physics?

November 2-9, 1931

The week of November 2-9 will be devoted to study and discussion of biological evolution. Each student is requested to read G. H. Parker, *What Evolution Is.*

The paper, which is due at 8 o'clock, Monday, November 9, is to be on the subject, "Is Evolution True?"

Mr. Havighurst, or any of the other advisers, will suggest extra reading on evolution for those desiring it. Those who find the Parker fairly easy reading are advised to read Baitsell, *Evolution of Earth and Man.*

October, 1931
Memorandum on Regional Studies

Objectives:

Every student ought to gain from his regional study a clearer understanding of his particular community—in terms of its physical basis, its historical development and changing character, its present-day practices, values, and problems. Each author should seek not merely to describe his community but also to interpret and appraise it (hence data should not be merely listed, but rather used and explained in terms of their significance). Each study may well raise in the author's mind more questions than he can answer, but such problems are worth formulating and may well be included in the completed paper. The value of each regional study should lie not merely in doing (as well as limited time, materials, and other studies permit) a given piece of intellectual work, not only in gaining more knowledge and awareness of one particular community, but also in the student's increased ability to understand and evaluate any concrete situation that he may confront in American life.

Scope:

Each paper must include some account of the physical characteristics and historical development of the region—as background essential to an understanding of the modern community.

Such basic factors as location, natural resources, means of communication, etc. (changing in character and importance with changing technology), should clearly be treated to some extent in every study. (See Lobeck's *Physiographic Diagram*, J. Russell Smith's *North America*, and other physical and economic geographies.) Maps and charts can be used to advantage in presenting much of this material on the wider area within which your community is located.

Of course these physical factors are relevant only in view of the people who have come to the region—at different times, from other countries or regions, with varying motives, cultural backgrounds, and economic skills. How did the place and the people interact, and what kind of a society gradually emerged? How does this process of growth and development throw light on the community of today (toward which your whole study points and with which it is mainly concerned)?

Each study should also include:

Either a general survey and appraisal of various phases of life in the region, as in *Middletown*—(probably possible only where the student is dealing with a fairly small and familiar community);

Or a more intensive study of one aspect—in which the student is especially interested and in which the life of the region is significantly revealed. (Of course any such aspect will touch and should throw light on the general situation at many points.)

Note: Quite a wide variation between individual regional studies (as to scope, content, organization, emphasis, treatment, style, etc.) is naturally possible under (and consistent with) the above general requirements. In fact, each study will (and should) reveal the background and values of the author as well as those of his region.

Procedure:

By this time, each student ought to have selected his region, to have collected some material for his study, to have decided what special phase or phases he plans to emphasize, and to have consulted with his present adviser on this program.

The regional study is to be carried on by each student throughout the entire semester along with the other work regularly scheduled for the whole group. In other words, as the year's schedule now stands, no solid time (free from college meetings and assignments) will be available for the regional studies, except for the final exam period from January 25 until the papers are due on February 8. Each student is reponsible for planning his own work accordingly. For the conference just before the Christmas recess, each student should line up his study to see what gaps are left and what work remains to be done, in order to discuss this situation with his adviser. (He may, of course, consult with his adviser at any time during the semester.)

Two copies, typed, are to be handed in with whatever maps, illustrations, or charts you may find useful. You should attach a bibliography in which you evaluate critically the materials you have consulted, pointing out those of value and those not of value as a guide to the reader; your footnotes and quotations should also be used to aid the reader (and should follow the printed "instruction sheet" available in the college office); and a table of contents should be given. Finally, you are to attach a statement in which you set forth your criticisms and impressions and suggestions concerning the regional study assignment and any record of your attitude as it developed during the progress of your work.

Sophomore Year
Book List
1931-1932

Architecture:

Louis Sullivan, *Autobiography of an Idea*

Autobiography and Biography:

Henry Adams, *The Education of Henry Adams*
Jane Addams, *Twenty Years at Hull House*
Mrs. Chesnut, *A Diary from Dixie*
Ralph Waldo Emerson, *Letters*
        The Heart of Emerson's Journals,
         ed. by Bliss Perry
Hamlin Garland, *A Son of the Middle Border*
James G. Huneker, *Steeplejack*
William James, *Letters*
James Weldon Johnson, *The Autobiography of an Ex-Colored Man*
Ernest L. Meyer, *Hey! Yellowbacks*
John Muir, *The Story of My Boyhood and Youth*
Lee Sage, *The Last Rustler*
Carl Sandburg, *Abraham Lincoln*
Mark Twain, *Life on the Mississippi*
      Roughing It
Booker T. Washington, *Up from Slavery*
Walt Whitman, *Letters*

Class Assignments

Economics:

Stuart Chase, *Mexico*
> *The Tragedy of Waste*

W. E. Dodd, *The Cotton Kingdom*

Henry George, *Progress and Poverty*

Selig Perlman, *History of American Trade Unionism*
> *Theory of the Labor Movement*

Ida Tarbell, *The History of the Standard Oil Company* (2 vols.)

Thorstein Veblen, *A Theory of the Leisure Class*

Education:

Alexander Meiklejohn, *Freedom and the College*
> *The Liberal College*

History:

Frederick Jackson Turner, *The Frontier in American History*

Abraham Lincoln, *State Papers*

Samuel E. Morison, *The Maritime History of Massachusetts*

Francis Parkman, *The Oregon Trail*

History and Literary Criticism:

E. E. Parrington, *Main Currents in American Thought*

Nature and Man:

H. D. Thoreau, *Walden*

Novels:

Sherwood Anderson, *Many Marriages*

Johan Bojer, *The Emigrants*

James Boyd, *Drums*

Willa Cather, *Death Comes for the Archbishop*
> *O Pioneers!*

Stephen Crane, *The Red Badge of Courage*

E. E. Cummings, *The Enormous Room*

John Dos Passos, *Manhattan Transfer*

Theodore Dreiser, *An American Tragedy*

Louis Hemon, *Maria Chapdelaine*

La Farge, *Laughing Boy*
Sinclair Lewis, *Arrowsmith*
        Babbitt
        Main Street
Herman Melville, *White Jacket*
Julia Peterkin, *Black April*
        Scarlet Sister Mary
O. E. Rölvaag, *Giants in the Earth*
Upton Sinclair, *Boston*
Harriet Beecher Stowe, *Uncle Tom's Cabin*
Mark Twain, *Huckleberry Finn*
Owen Wister, *The Virginian*
Edith Wharton, *Ethan Frome*

Philosophy:

John Dewey, *Human Nature and Conduct*
William James, *Pragmatism*
M. C. Otto, *Things and Ideals*

Plays:

E. E. Cummings, *Him*
Eugene O'Neill, *The Hairy Ape*

Poetry:

Stephen Vincent Benet, *John Brown's Body*
Emily Dickinson, *Poems*
Robert Frost, *Poems*
Robinson Jeffers, *Poems*
James Weldon Johnson, *God's Trombones*
Edna St. Vincent Millay, *Poems*
Walt Whitman, *Poems*

Short Stories:

Sherwood Anderson, *Winesburg, Ohio*
Theodore Dreiser, *Chains*
Ernest Hemingway, *Men Without Women*

The State and Man:

L. D. Brandeis, *Business, a Profession*

Class Assignments

Opinions
Other People's Money
O. W. Holmes, Dissenting Opinions
Abraham Lincoln, Speeches
Walter Lippmann, Public Opinion
Woodrow Wilson, Collected Addresses

November 12, 1931
Ninteenth-Century American Democracy

For three weeks, beginning Thursday, November 12, we shall approach nineteenth-century America as students of the problems of statecraft. Our most important book will be the *Education of Henry Adams*. During this period we shall read this book with one purpose uppermost: to understand the society which Adams watched so critically and to derive from him whatever help we can in interpretation and judgment. Since we shall be chiefly concerned with one phase of Adams's thought, we shall not find all chapters equally relevant. Nevertheless, one of our aims in this period is to acquaint ourselves with the *Education* itself, and everyone is asked to read the book carefully from beginning to end. For further enlightenment you should read the designated chapters in Beard's *Rise of American Civilization*. The advisers will give you additional reading suggestions.

College meetings will be, as usual, at 10 o'clock in the New Soils Building. Meetings devoted to historical analyses will precede meetings in which general issues arising from the historical situations will be discussed. All of the issues will be concerned with phases of the question: What is the individual's relation to the group?

The meetings will be as follows:

Thursday, November 12, Early Nineteenth-Century New England—Adams, 1-4; Beard, 8-10.

Friday, November 13, Jacksonian Democracy—Beard, 11-16.

Tuesday, November 17, Was the Puritan outlook a valid approach to life in nineteenth-century America?

159

Wednesday, November 18, Slavery Controversy—Adams, 5-7; Beard, 17.

Thursday, November 19, Was the slavery dispute a moral conflict?

Friday, November 20, Diplomacy of the Civil War—Adams 8-15; Beard, 18.

Tuesday, November 24, What are "principles" in international affairs?

Wednesday, November 25, Post-Civil War Politics—Adams 16-20; Beard, 20, 23, 25.

Friday, November 27, Do you approve of Adams's attitude toward post-Civil War Politics?

Tuesday, December 1, Post-Civil War Currency Situation—Adams, 21-23; Beard, 23.

Wednesday, December 2, Where lay social justice in the currency issue?

Thursday, December 3, The Progressive Movement—Adams, 24; Beard, 27.

Friday, December 4, Are the principles of progressive democracy adequate for a modern political philosophy?

There will be an announcement on the bulletin board concerning the papers to be written.

Book List for the Study
of Nineteenth-Century America

There are four important large-scale United States histories whose various volumes, chronologically arranged, will give you information on particular situations. Their authors and scopes are as follows:

Adams, Henry, 9 vols. 1800-1817. Good for political and international affairs.

Channing, Edward, 6 vols. 1700-1865. Good especially for colonial history.

McMaster, J. B., 8 vols. 1783-1861. Good for general social description.

Rhodes, J. F., 9 vols. 1849-1909. Good for slave question, Civil War, and reconstruction.

There are also three important series of books by specialists on separate periods or topics:

Hart, A. B. (ed.), *American Nation*, 28 vols. 1600-1917.

Johnson, Allen (ed.), *Chronicles of America*, 50 vols. 1492-1920.

Schlesinger and Fox (eds.), *History of American Life*, 12 vols. 1600-1930.

For special references consult Channing, Hart, and Turner, *Guide to American History*. This is a detailed outline of American history with bibliographies under all headings.

The following books are specially recommended for our purposes:

Early Nineteenth-Century New England:

Adams, Henry, *History of the United States*, Vols. I, IX
    Degradation of Democratic Dogma
Adams, James T., *Adams Family*
    New England in the Republic
Becker, Carl, *Declaration of Independence*
Morison, S. E., *Maritime History of Massachusetts*
Parrington, V.L., *Main Currents in American Thought*

Jacksonian Democracy:

Fish, C. R., *Rise of the Common Man*
Paxson, F. L., *History of the American Frontier*
Schlesinger, Arthur, *New Viewpoints in American History*
Tocqueville, Alexis de, *Democracy in America*, Vol. II
Turner, F. J., *Frontier in American History*
Turner, F. J., *Rise of the New West*

Slavery Controversy:

Becker, Carl, *Declaration of Independence*
Dodd, William E., *Cotton Kingdom*
Lincoln, A., *Letters and Speeches*
Macy, J., *Anti-Slavery Crusade*
Parrington, V.L., *Main Currents in American Thought*, Vol. II
Rhodes, James F., *History of the United States*, Vols. I, II

Diplomacy during and after the Civil War:

Adams, E. D., *Great Britain and the American Civil War*
Adams, J. T., *Adams Family*
Foster, *Century of American Diplomacy*
Rhodes, James F., *History of the United States*, Vol. IV
Thayer, W. R., *Life and Letters of John Hay*, Vol. II

Post-Civil War Politics:

Adams, Henry, *Democracy*
Beard, C. A., *Contemporary American History*
Bryce, James, *American Commonwealth*, Vol. II
Paxson, F. L., *Recent United States History*

Post-Civil War Currency Situation:

Beard, C. A., *Contemporary American History*
Buck, Solon J., *Agrarian Crusade*
Sullivan, Mark, *Our Times*, Vol. I.
Turner, F. J., *Frontier in American History*

Progressive Movement:

De Witt, B. P., *Progressive Movement*
Faulkner, Harold N., *Quest for Social Justice*
La Follette, R.M., *Autobiography*

Idea of Democracy:

Abbott, Lyman, *Spirit of Democracy*
Croly, H., *Promise of American Life*
Dewey, John, *The Public and Its Problems*
Fite, Warner, *Individualism*
Follette, M. P., *The New State*, Pt. II
Hadley, A. T., *Freedom and Responsibility*
Lindsay, A.D., *Essentials of Democracy*
Smith, T. V., *American Philosophy of Equality*
Wright, H.W., *Moral Standards of Democracy*

November 16, 1931

"We hold these truths to be self-evident, that all men are created equal, that they are endowed by their Creator with certain unalienable Rights, that among these are Life, Liberty, and the pursuit of Happiness. That to secure these rights, Governments are instituted among Men, deriving their just powers from the consent of the governed . . . ."

Paper, due December 7:

The nineteenth-century development of America is commonly regarded as the working out of the principles embodied in this statement. Describe and discuss each episode we have considered, and show how far these principles were involved. Do you think the series of episodes shows any consistent movement toward or away from these principles? Do you think the statement as quoted from the Declaration of Independence is adequate for a modern political philosophy? If not, what revisions or substitutions can you offer?

December 7-14, 1931

Reading:

You are asked to read carefully (1) Governor LaFollette's November 24 message to the legislature, and (2) the printed report of the Wisconsin Interim Committee on Unemployment—both available free in the college office. These documents are to serve as a background for the "hearings" of the legislature and for our discussion of the unemployment problem. Other reading along these lines will be suggested in college meetings or by your adviser.

Meetings:

Tuesday, December 8—The assembly (committee of the whole) will hold a hearing on Bill No. 8A—"Unemployment Reserves and Compensation." Both sides will be presented. You are asked to attend these sessions, in the gallery of the assembly.

Wednesday, December 9, 10 o'clock—New Soils Building. College meeting for discussion of the problem and the evidence presented at Tuesday's hearing.

2 o'clock—The Senate Committee on Agriculture and Labor will hold hearings on two unemployment bills. All

members of the college are asked to listen carefully to the arguments presented for and against these two bills.

Thursday, December 10, 10 o'clock—New Soils Building. College meeting.

Friday, December 11, 10 o'clock—New Soils Building. College meeting.

(On either Thursday or Friday morning we hope to have a representative "conservative" discuss with us his views on unemployment and the governor's proposals.)

Paper, due December 14:

Discuss the relation between Wisconsin's unemployment problem and American "democracy." (What implications, if any, has democracy for the solution of this economic question?) In the second part of your paper, discuss the economic facts and elements to be taken account of in attempting to deal with Wisconsin's immediate or long run unemployment problems.

Note: The week of December 14-18 will be devoted to a study of "The Case of Bituminous Coal," which likewise raises significant issues bearing on our whole economic situation.

December 14-18, 1931

Reading:

Hamilton and Wright, *The Case of Bituminous Coal*

Meetings:

Monday, Tuesday, Wednesday, Thursday to discuss problems raised by the reading.

January 11-16, 1932

A brief paper dealing with some aspect of the "public control of business" will be due from each student by Monday noon, January 18, unless the student has previously made a substitute arrangement with his adviser. (Several of the groups are taking special topics for group discussion and presenting individual papers in that connection.)

The following are suggested as possible topics:

The background, purposes, and provisions of (one or more of) the three major antitrust laws; the work of the Federal Trade Commission as revealed in its annual reports; specific unfair business practices; trade associations; industry planning (the Swope Plan and the Harriman Report); national planning (as discussed in testimony before Senator La Follette's Senate sub-committee); conditions under which a business is so "affected with a public interest" that price regulation is economically and/or legally justified; present limits on the effective regulation of public utilities; the problems of administration involved in the public control of business; government competition as a means of control; any other topic growing fairly directly out of the week's general reading, subject to the adviser's approval; or, alternatively, the economic facts and legal-economic issues in any *one* of the following legal cases:

The *Standard Oil Company* case (1911); the *U.S. Steel Corporation* case (1920); the earlier *United Shoe Machinery* case (1918); the *Maple Flooring Association* case (1925); the *Duplex Printing Press Company* case (1921); the *Bedford Stone Company* case (1927); the *Wolff Packing Company* case (1923); the *Tyson and Brothers* case (1927); the *Ribnik* case (1928); the *State of Missouri ex rel. Southwestern Bell Telephone Co.* case (1923); *St. Louis and O'Fallon* case (1929); *Green v. Frazier* (1920). (To locate any of these cases, see the footnote reference to U.S. Supreme Court decisions in the *Public Control of Business.*)

January 18-25, 1932

The book to be studied this week is *Other People's Money*, by Louis D. Brandeis.

A brief paper dealing with some aspect of this book will be due from each student by 10 o'clock Monday morning, January 25. Suggested topics: The structure of the "money trust"; the importance of "interlocking directorates"; the function of the investment banker; the *New Haven Railroad* case; financing government borrowing by government agency; the possible role of publicity.

College Meetings:

Monday, Tuesday, Wednesday, Thursday, Friday.

January 25-30, 1932

The book to be studied by all the college will be *The Acquisitive Society*, by R. H. Tawney.

During this week each member of the college (including advisers) will be asked to join one of three groups, respectively, for "capitalism," "socialism," or "communism." Each of these groups will meet for the purpose of working out and stating its position. Each group will then delegate representatives to explain and urge its point of view before the general college meetings during the latter part of the week.

Over the weekend, therefore, each student should try to define his own position, and (by Monday morning) decide which group to join for the week's discussions.

Every student should write and hand in a brief paper either formulating his own present position or analyzing Tawney's conception of a "functional society."

College Meetings:

Monday, Tuesday, Wednesday, Thursday, Friday, largely under the discussion of Mr. Meiklejohn.

Sophomore Literature Period
1932

During the literature period there will be two concurrent undertakings. One of these is to be the reading and discussion of four books:

An American Tragedy by Theodore Dreiser. *John Brown's Body* by Stephen Vincent Benet. *Manhattan Transfer* by

John Dos Passos. *Black April* by Julia Peterkin.

The other undertaking will be the group-studies made by each adviser with his advisees. The advisers announce the subjects of these studies as follows:

Carl Boghölt—"Walt Whitman"

(What did this Barbarian yawp about? What difference has it made?)

H. H. Giles—"Byron, Keats, and Shelley; T. S. Eliot and Others"

(A study of the romanticists and their belief in the fullness of life as opposed to the modern tendency to seek escape from life in irony and obscurity.)

Robert Havighurst—"The Middle West in Literature"

(The group will make a study of novelists and poets who have attempted to interpret the Middle West. Each student will study the work of some writer who has written about the Middle West and who interests him particularly.

Alexander Meiklejohn—"Dreiser, Dos Passos, Peterkin"

(Reading of other books by the same or related authors. A study of some contemporary novels in terms of the social ideas and attitudes which they express.)

D. Otis—"Sherwood Anderson"

John Powell—"Criticism"

(The group will study criticism, in the persons of certain critics and in the pages of certain magazines, and will attempt (a) to define the character and aims of the critical activity, and (b) to bring into view the approaches and the values of different groups of critics. The men who will be studied by members of this group are: Krutch (*Modern Temper*, etc.), Van Doren, Lawrence (*Studies; Pansies*), Mumford (*Golden Day; Melville*), Bourne, Sherman (*Points of View*, etc.), Foerster (*Humanism in America*), Mencken (books; and

167

Mercury, 1931), Young (books; and New Republic for 1931), Wilson (New Republic for 1930-31), Canby (Saturday Review), Eliot (Criticism in America; etc.))

Assignments to groups will be made as usual. It is important to note, however, that in any case where a student wishes to work on the project of another group than that to which he is assigned, he is free to exchange membership with anyone who wishes to do so.

February 8-May 1, 1931*

We have found, as did Henry Adams, that to understand modern America we must have some appreciation of the factors that profoundly modified the older classical and medieval civilizations. The methods and content of scientific study, expanding from physical, mathematical, and astronomical investigations into the study of plant and animal life, are now invading the study of human behavior and of social institutions. Vast areas of the earth's surface have been discovered and brought within a system of world communication. As a result, we have created a new institutional system in our finance, industry, politics, morals, and religion. Even ancient societies outside the earlier centers of western Christendom, such as Russia, China, Japan, and India, are profoundly affected by these changes.

As this new society attempts to interpret and appraise itself in literature and the arts, in religion and philosophy, and to find new enjoyments and values of life, we shall find the same influences at work and a corresponding transformation taking place.

Here again we shall initiate our inquiry in terms of the society which immediately surrounds us—that of the United States. We shall first study directly the appraisals made by a few men and women of unusual experience, sensitivity, or

---

*Because the assignments for the last months of the year 1931-32 are not available, those for the corresponding months of 1930-31 have been substituted.

168

achievement; we shall then try to see this world through the eyes of the artist—because of practical limitations of equipment, we shall turn to the novelist, poet, and dramatist. Following the first of May, we shall study the effort of the philosopher, the moralist, and the religious teacher to appraise and evaluate the worth of life in this rapidly changing society.

Henry Adams shared with some intimacy in all—and more—of these kinds of experience during his lifetime. Any effort to understand what he is saying, and write about it intelligently, therefore, requires a conscious and determined effort to approach life in the Great Society through as many kinds of experience as we can. Naturally, to each one of us, some one of these approaches is of most interest. A lifetime of effort and study is required if one would have any success at all in acquiring its techniques and mastering its fundamentals; but this does not entirely disbar us from seeing what the significance and values of other approaches than our own are.

From February 9 to March 1, we will study the memoirs here listed, of which you are required to read at least three. You will find most of these available in one or more reprint libraries at from fifty cents to one dollar in price. The *Letters of William James* is more expensive, but you are strongly urged to buy it and read it. You will find it an increasingly valuable resource through the years. The same applies to *The Heart of Emerson's Journals*. You often can pick up these books cheaply on bargain counters in town or in Chicago or in second-hand bookshops.

Memoirs—at least three to be selected for special study:

Franklin, *Autobiography*; Lincoln, *Selected Papers* (Scribner edition); *The Heart of Emerson's Journals*; Thoreau's *Walden*; John Muir, *The Story of My Boyhood and Youth*; Mark Twain, *Life on the Mississippi* and *Roughing it*; W. Wilson, *Addresses and Messages*; *The Autobiography of Andrew Carnegie*; Henry Ford, *My Life and Work*; Mary Antin, *The Promised Land*; Panunzio, *The Soul of an Immigrant*; Edward Bok, *The Americanization of Edward Bok*; Carl Jensen, *An American*

Saga; Booker Washington, *Up from Slavery*; Jane Addams, *Twenty Years at Hull House*; *The Letters of Henry James*; *The Letters of William James*; Louis Sullivan, *The Autobiography of an Idea*; *The Reminiscences of Raphael Pumpelly* (geologist, mining engineer, traveller); Cecelia Beaux, *Background with Figures*. It is suggested that you discuss your selections with your adviser before making a final choice. It is possible that some memoirs not on this list will be thought suitable for substitution.

During March, we shall devote our time especially to group or individual studies in literature or the arts. All members of the class should read, in addition, the following novels:

Cather, *My Antonia* or *O Pioneers!*; Wharton, *The Age of Innocence* or *The House of Mirth*; Jewett, *The Country of the Pointed Firs*; Peterkin, *Scarlet Sister Mary*; Hergesheimer, *Java Head* or *The Three Black Pennys*; Hemingway, *The Sun Also Rises*; Lewis, *Arrowsmith*.

Here again, you may profitably consult with your adviser and possibly make substitutions, although it seems desirable to have a common sharing of acquaintance with the view of American life which these artists convey and with the aspects of technique and presentation which they reflect.

John M. Gaus.

February, 1931

Paper, due March 1:

A critical essay on one of the men or women whose autobiography you have read. Include some consideration of the light thrown upon the development of an American civilization as seen through these memoirs and other reading.

April 6, 1931

The final paper on *The Education of Henry Adams* will be due on May 6 at 4 P.M. Papers handed in after that time will not be acceptable as a basis for determining the final grade of the student.

It will be recalled that these papers are designed to constitute extended reviews of the book with special emphasis upon two points. Each paper should contain a clear and coherent discussion of the argument of the book; in light of the studies of the year in science, social institutions, history and memoirs, literature, and any other relevant topics, comment upon the events and situations presented by Adams. Each paper should also present a thorough and critical study of some phase of Adams's thought, observations, or interests which seems to the writer especially significant or important or which has some special interest for the writer. Just as the first task relates the preparation of the paper to all of the work of the year, the second naturally implies the study and discussion of other books related to the special field of interest. This paper is really a study of the emergence of modern America in particular and the modern world in general.

There will be sophomore meetings during the period, April 15-May 6, at which various advisers will discuss some aspect of *The Education of Henry Adams.*

May 7, 1931
Philosophy

We may conceive of the work of the past two years as a study of the attempt of two widely different groups of people to conduct an ordered and successful social life. Their arrangements for producing goods and sharing in their consumption, their modes of government, their social institutions, art, and science, all have been the subjects of our investigation. The study of fifth-century Athens soon revealed the presence in the society of men who criticized existing arrangements and deplored their effects upon the welfare of the group. The most important of these critics of

Greek society was, of course, Plato, whose reflections upon man and society resulted in a view of human nature and conduct which has influenced thought about these matters ever since.

Likewise, we have found modern industrial America has its critics; and the literature devoted to the criticism of existing institutions is increasing in volume. Many of the views expressed, however, leave unexamined the view of human nature and intelligence, (its nature and function) which serves as their basis. It will be our purpose during the remaining weeks of the year to make as careful and critical a study as possible of one of these views—one that has had wide acceptance during the last twenty years. The book that will be used in this study is John Dewey's *Human Nature and Conduct*. Every student should arrange to have a copy of the book available for his use.

Additional books suggested for use in group discussions:
Lippmann, Walter, *Preface to Morals*; Krutch, J.W., *The Modern Temper*; Fite, Warner, *Moral Philosophy*; Meiklejohn, Alexander, *Philosophy*; Otto, M.C., *Things and Ideals* and *Natural Laws and Human Hopes*; Plato, *Gorgias, Republic*; Tawney, *The Acquisitive Society*; Zimmern, Alfred, *Learning and Leadership*.

Carl M. Bogholt.

Bibliography

Bibliography*

I. Works by Alexander Meiklejohn
A. Major Books

Education Between Two Worlds. New York: Harper & Brothers, 1942.

The Experimental College. New York: Harper & Brothers, 1932.

Freedom and the College. New York: The Century Co., 1923.

Free Speech and Its Relation to Self-Government. New York: Harper & Brothers, 1948.

Inclinations and Obligations. Berkeley: University of California Press, 1948.

The Liberal College. Boston: Marshall Jones Co., 1920.

Political Freedom: The Constitutional Powers of the People. New York: Harper & Brothers, 1948.

B. Articles (in chronological order)

Review of *La modalite du jugement*, by Leon Brunschvicg. *Philosophical Review* 6(1897): 677-79.

Review of *Les principles du positivisme contemporain*, by Jean Halleux. *Philosophical Review* 8(1899): 212-13.

Review of *The Relation of Berkeley's Later to His Earlier Idealism*, by Carl V. Tower. *Philosophical Review* 10(1901): 102-04.

Review of *A Syllabus of an Introduction to Philosophy*, by Walter G. Marvin. *Philosophical Review* 10(1901): 322-24.

Review of *Kant contra Haeckel*, by Von Erich Adickes. *Philosophical Review* 10(1901): 668-70.

"Evils of College Athletics." *Harpers* 49(1905): 1751-52.

*Selected from James Milborn Green's Ph.D. dissertation, "Alexander Meiklejohn: Innovator in Undergraduate Education," University of Michigan, 1970-71.

"College Education and the Moral Ideal." *Education* 28 (1908): 552-67.

"Is Mental Training a Myth?" *Educational Review* 37(1909): 126-41.

"Are College Entrance Requirements Excessive?" *Education* 29(1909): 561-66.

"Competition in College." *Brown Alumni Monthly* 10(1909): 75-78.

"Fraternities and Sororities." *Brown Alumni Monthly* 11 (1910): 89-91.

"What Constitutes Preparation for College." *Education* 31 (1911): 578-84.

"Values of Logic and the College Curriculum." *Religious Education* 7(1912): 62-68.

"Inaugural Address: Aim of College Education." *Amherst Graduates' Quarterly* 2(1912): 56-73.

Reprinted in *The Liberal College; Freedom and the College; Essays for College Men,* edited by N. Foerster. New York: Henry Holt & Co.

"Baccalaureate Address." *The Amherst Student,* 21 June, 1913; 23 June 1914; 29 June 1915; 20 June 1916; and 19 June 1917.

"The Goals and the Game." *Amherst Graduates' Quarterly* 3(1913): 11-20.

"Report of the President to the Trustees." *Amherst College Bulletin* 3(1914): 3.

Reprinted in part in *The Liberal College,* pp. 135-48.

"Purpose of the Liberal College." *National Education Association, Proceedings and Addresses,* 1914, pp. 102-03.

"Liberal Education." *Kindergarten Primary Magazine* 27 (1914): 2.

"Place of Student Activities." *Education* 35(1915): 312-19.

"Address at Inauguration of Hermon C. Bumpus as President of Tufts College." *Tufts College Graduate* 14 (1915): 69-75.

"Schoolmaster's View of Compulsory Military Training." *School and Society* 4(1916): 9-14.

"Fiat Justitai—The College As Critic." *Harvard Graduate Magazine* 26(1917): 1-14.

Reprinted in *The Liberal College.*

"Chapel Address." *Amherst Graduates' Quarterly* 7(1917): 8-12.

"Freedom of the College." *Atlantic* 121(1918): 83-89.

Reprinted in *The Liberal College,* pp. 84-96.

"The Last Two Years of the College Course." *Association of American Colleges Bulletin* 24(1918): 22-32.

"Keep On in College." *Christian Education World* 18 July 1918, p. 811.

"Colleges and the S.A.T.C." *Nation* 107(1918): 697-98.

"Report of the President to the Trustees." *Amherst College Bulletin* 8(1918): 1.

Reprinted in part in *The Liberal College,* pp. 149-63; *Freedom and the College,* pp. 207-31.

"The Four-Year American Cultural College." *Proceedings of the Thirty-third Annual Convention of the Association of Colleges and Preparatory Schools of the Middle States and Maryland,* 1919, pp. 48-60.

"Future of Our Liberal Colleges." *New York Sun,* 19 October 1919.

"English Impressions." *Amherst Graduates' Quarterly* 9(1919): 7-11.

"Production, Distribution and Use." *Proceedings of the Fifth Annual Meeting, the Association of Urban Universities,* 1919, pp. 54-60.

"The Trustees." *Amherst Graduates' Quarterly* 10 (1920): 24-25.

"What Does Amherst Hope To Be During the Next Hundred Years?" *Amherst Graduates' Quarterly* 10 (1921): 327-47.

Reprinted in *Freedom and the College.*

"For Athletic Disarmament." *Amherst Graduates' Quarterly* 11 (1922): 171-73.

An address delivered before the New York Alumni Association on 17 February 1922. Reprinted as "Intercollegiate Athletics." *Outdoor* 130(1922): 387.

"Unity of the Curriculum." *New Republic* 32(1922): supplement 2-3.

Reprinted in *Freedom and the College*, pp. 193-203.

"What Are College Games For?" *Atlantic* 130(1922): 663-71.

Reprinted in *Freedom and the College*, pp. 71-97.

"Democracy Held Success, Not a Popular Delusion." *New York Times*, 17 December 1922, p. 2.

"The Measure of a College." *Amherst Graduates' Quarterly* 12 (1923): 85-92.

"Unifying the Liberal Arts Curriculum." *Association of American Colleges Bulletin* 9(1923): 79-90.

"What American Education Lacks." *Columbia: Knights of Columbus*, May 1923, p. 6.

"Pharisees and Reformers." *Nation* 117(1923): 13.

"Farewell Address at Amherst Alumni Luncheon." *School and Society* 18(1923): 12-16.

"Is Our World Christian?" *Amherst Graduates' Quarterly* 12(1923): 224-233.

Reprinted in *Freedom and the College*.

"Letter of Resignation." *Amherst Graduates' Quarterly* 12(1923): 219-20.

"To Whom Are We Responsible?" *Century* 106(1923): 643-50.

Reprinted in *Freedom and the College*, pp. 3-23.

"Colleges and the Common Life." *Harpers* 147(1923): 721-26.

Reprinted in *Essays Toward Truth* edited by K. H. Robinson et al., p. 3-14.

"Devils Revenge." *Century* 107(1924): 718-23.

"A New College, Notes on a Next Step in Higher Education." *Century* 109(1925): 312-20.

"Philosophers and Others." *Philosophical Review* 34(1925): 262-80.

"Woodrow Wilson, Teacher." *Saturday Review of Literature* 1(1925): 785-86.

"A New College." *New Republic* 46(1926): 215-18.

"A New College With a New Idea." *New York Times Magazine*, 29 May 1927, p. 1.

"Wisconsin's Experimental College." *Survey* 58(1927): 268-70.

"The Experimental College." *Bulletin of the University of Wisconsin*, serial no. 1454, general series no. 1230, June 1927.

"From the Chairman to the Students." In *The First Year of the Experimental College*, pp. 45-48. Madison: The Pioneer Class of the Experimental College, 1928.

"The Experimental College." *Bulletin of the University of Wisconsin*, serial no. 1510, general series no. 1284, March 1928.

"The Experimental College." *The Wisconsin Alumni Magazine*, April 1928, p. 237.

"In Memoriam." *New Republic* 56(1928): 69-71.

"The Experimental College After a Year." *Wisconsin Journal of Education* 61(1928): 14-16.

Reprinted in *Chicago School Journal* 11(1929): 201-04.

"The Experimental College." *Bulletin of the University of Wisconsin*, serial no. 1555, general series no. 1329, October 1928.

"Who Should Go to College?" *New Republic* 57(1929): 238-41.

"What Next in Progressive Education?" *Progressive Education* 6 (1929): 99-110.

Reprinted in *Higher Education Faces the Future*, edited by P. A. Schilpp, pp. 289-307. New York: Horace Liveright, 1930.

"Educational Leadership in America." *Harpers* 160(1930): 440-47.

Revised form of address given at commencement, Reed College.

"Philosophers Join in a Plea for Peace." *New York Times,* 7 September 1930, sec. 3, p. 4.

"What We Ought to Think About." *The Executives' Club News* 7(1930): 4-8.

"Wisconsin's Experimental College." *Journal of Higher Education* 1(1930): 485-90.

"Rejoinder." *Nation* 132(1931): 325-26.

"Some Notes on the Techniques of Experimentation in a Liberal College." In *Changes and Experiments in Liberal Arts Education, Thirty-first Yearbook of the National Society for the Study of Education, Part II,* pp. 213-20. Bloomington, IL: Public School Publishing Co., 1932.

"The Reorganization of Content to Emphasize Fields of Learning or the Relation of Branches of Knowledge." In *Changes and Experiments in Liberal Arts Education,* pp. 162-64. Bloomington, IL: Public School Publishing Co., 1932.

"Letter of Greeting to President Stanley King." *Amherst Graduates' Quarterly* 73(1932): 12.

"Adult Education: A Fresh Start." *New Republic* 80(1934): 14-17.

"Liberty For What?" *Harpers* 171(1935): 364-72.

Foreword to *Selected Supreme Court Decisions,* edited by Mayer Cohen. New York: Harper & Brothers, 1937.

"Teachers and Controversial Questions." *Harpers* 177(1938): 22.

"Must America Change Its Theory of Civil Liberties?" *Vital Speeches* 6(1940): 720-24.

"Higher Education in a Democracy." *North Central Association Quarterly* 16(1941): 149-154.

"The Meaning of a College." In *Living and Learning, Proceedings of an Anniversary in Honor of Alexander Meiklejohn,* edited by Walter H. Hill. Chicago: Walter H. Hill, 1942.

"Congress and the People." *Nation,* 155(1942): 469-71.

"Future of Liberal Education." *New Republic* 108(1943): 113-15.

"For International Citizenship." *Adult Education Journal* 2(1943): 44-47.

"Education as a Factor in Post-War Reconstruction." *Free World* 5(1943): 27-31.

"Teacher, Teach Thyself." *Adult Education Journal* 2(1943): 120-29.

"Reason or Violence." *Common Sense* 12(1943): 283-86.

"Mr. Hutchins' Dogma." *New Republic* 109(1943): 147-48.

"Required Education for Freedom." *American Scholar* 13(1944): 393-95.

"Reply to John Dewey." *Fortune* 31(1945): 207.

"Rejoinder." *Fortune* 31(1945): 14.

"Education Under the Charter." *Free World* 10(1945): 37-39.

"To Teach the World How to Be Free." *New York Times Magazine*, 11 August 1946, p. 5.

"Everything Worth Saying Should Be Said." *New York Times Magazine*, 18 July 1948, p. 8.

"Should Communists Be Allowed to Teach." *New York Times Magazine*, 27 March 1949, p. 10.

"Educational Cooperation Between Church and State." Law and *Contemporary Problems, Journal of Duke University School of Law* 14(1949): 61-72.

"The First Amendment and the Evils Congress Has a Right to Prevent." *Indiana Law Journal* 26(1951): 10-25.

"The Teaching of Intellectual Freedom." *Bulletin of the American Association of University Professors* 38(1952): 10-25.

"The Crisis in Freedom." *Progressive* 16(1952): 15-18.

"Food for Thought." *Spectator* 189(1952): 58-59.

"Integrity of the University: How to Defend It." *Bulletin of Atomic Science* 9(1953): 193-94.

"What Does the First Amendment Mean?" *University of Chicago Law Review* 20(1953): 461-79.

"The Limits of Congressional Authority: Freedom and the People." *Nation* 177(1953): 500-03.

"Letter." *Harvard Crimson*, January 1954.

"Sedition Circa 400 B.C." *Nation* 180(1955): 349-52.

"Testimony on the Meaning of the First Amendment." Hennings Subcommittee on Constitutional Rights of the Senate Judiciary Committee, 4 November 1956.

"The American College and American Freedom." Washington: United States Printing Office, 10 May 1957.

"Chapel Address, 1957." *Amherst Alumni News* 10(1957): 3-5.

"The Legal Status of Our Freedom." *Law Guild Review* 10(1960): 106-08.

"The Barenblatt Opinion." *University of Chicago Law Review* 27 (1960): 329-40.

"First Amendment Is an Absolute." *Supreme Court Review* 45 (1961): 245-61.

"The Balancing of Self-Preservation Against Political Freedom." *California Law Review* 49(1961): 4-14.

"Words of Advice to the Graduates of Any Class at Any Time." *Bill of Rights Journal* 1(1968): 32-33. (published posthumously.)

II. Works about Alexander Meiklejohn
A. Articles

"Alexander Meiklejohn." *I.F. Stone Weekly*, 11 January 1965.

"Alexander Meiklejohn." *Nation* 199(1964): 506.

"Amherst College and President Meiklejohn." *School and Society* 17(1923): 687.

"Amherst's New President." *Review of Reviews* 46(1913): 15-16.

Corcoran, Thomas G. "The Militancy of Alexander Meiklejohn." *Brown Alumni Monthly* 65(1965): 12-15.

"Dr. Meiklejohn and the Issue of Academic Freedom." *Current Opinion* 75(1924): 212-14.

Bibliography

"Dr. Meiklejohn at Wisconsin." *Normal Instructor and Primary Plans* 35(1926): 6.

"Dr. Meiklejohn's Education Philosophy." *La Follett's Magazine*, February 1926, p. 29.

"Dr. Meiklejohn's Plan for a New College." *School and Society* 20(1924): 337-38.

"Dr. Meiklejohn Proposes." *New Republic* 41(1925): 246-48.

"Educational Reactionaries." *Literary Digest* 44(1912): 1256.

"Educator to Head Adult Research Center." *Newsweek* 2(1933): 16-17.

Everett, Walter. "Brown's Gift to Amherst." *Amherst Graduates' Quarterly* 2(1912-13): 148-53.

"Innovator." *Newsweek* 64(1964): 52.

"Learning's Mr. Different." *Newsweek* 49(1957): 114.

"Liberal Education." *School and Society* 18(1923): 27-28.

Lippmann, Walter. "The Fall of President Meiklejohn." *New York World*, 24 June 1923, Editorial Section, June 1923, p. 1.

Lovett, Robert M. "Meiklejohn of Amherst." *New Republic* 35(1923): 146-48.

Mayer, Milton. "Alec Meiklejohn's Maytime." *Progressive* 29(1965): 17-18.

"Meiklejohn at Seventy." *Newsweek* 19(1942): 56.

"Mid-America Revisited: Madison and Meiklejohn." *American Mercury* 8(1926): 323-25.

"Mild-Mannered Maverick." *Time* 69(1957): 67.

"Misplaced Man." *Freeman* 7(1923): 388-89.

"New President of Amherst." *Outlook* 101(1912): 669.

Pope, Arthur U. "Alexander Meiklejohn." *American Scholar*, 644 (Autumn 1965).

Price, Lucien, "Americans We Like: Alexander Meiklejohn." *Nation* 125(1927): 541-42.

Taylor, Harold. "Meiklejohn: The Art of Making People Think." *New York Times Magazine*, 5 May 1957, p. 20.

"Tribute to Alexander Meiklejohn." *American Association of University Professors Bulletin*, Autumn 1965, pp. 366-73.

III. Reviews of Books and Articles Written by Alexander Meiklejohn

Agard, William R. Review of *Freedom and the College*, by Alexander Meiklejohn. *Springfield Republican*, 11 November 1923, p. 7.

Ballou, Melvin C. Review of *Education Between Two Worlds*, by Alexander Meiklejohn. *Harvard Educational Review* 13(1943): 266-67.

Barr, Springfellow. Review of *Education Between Two Worlds*, by Alexander Meiklejohn. *Journal of Higher Education* 14(1943): 223.

Boucher, C.S. Review of *The Experimental College*, by Alexander Meiklejohn. *Journal of Higher Education* 4 (1933): 161.

Bode, Boyd H. Review of *Education Between Two Worlds*, by Alexander Meiklejohn. *Progressive Education* 19(1942): 445-46.

Duffus, Robert L. Review of *The Experimental College*, by Alexander Meiklejohn. *New York Times*, 19 June 1932, p. 5.

Erskine, John. Review of *The Experimental College*, by Alexander Meiklejohn. *Saturday Review of Literature* 8(1932): 813-14.

Hart, Joseph K. Review of *The Liberal College*, by Alexander Meiklejohn. *Survey* 45(1921): 545.

Heilman, Joseph K. "Light on a Darkling." Review of *Education Between Two Worlds*, by Alexander Meiklejohn. *Sewanee Review* 52(1944): 176-80.

Helsel, P. R. "Ideologies Motivating American Education: Discussion of Recent Articles in *Fortune* by John Dewey and Alexander Meiklejohn." *Personalist* 26(1945): 190-92.

Hook, Sidney. "Education for the New Order." Review of *Education Between Two Worlds*, by Alexander Meiklejohn. *Nation* 156(1943): 308-12.

Levi, Albert William. Review of *Education Between Two Worlds*, by Alexander Meiklejohn. *Ethics* 53(1943): 152-53.

Lewis, Hal G. "Meiklejohn and Experimentation." Review of *Education Between Two Worlds*, by Alexander Meiklejohn. *Teachers' College Record* 44(1943): 563-71.

McConn, Charles M. "How Shall We Educate the Barbarians? A Reply to Alexander Meiklejohn." *New Republic* 57(1929): 324-25.

Schneider, Herbert W. Review of *Education Between Two Worlds*, by Alexander Meiklejohn. *Journal of Philosophy* 39(1942): 689-95.

Smith, Preserved. Review of *The Liberal College*, by Alexander Meiklejohn. *The Nation* 111(1920): 734-35.

Whicher, George F. Review of *The Experimental College*, by Alexander Meiklejohn. *Books* 12 July 1932, p. 3.